# Over the Rocky Mountains to Alaska

## Charles Warren Stoddard

### Complete & Unabridged

Tutis Digital Publishing Private Limited

First published in 1914 as *Over the Rocky Mountains to Alaska.*

This edition published by
Tutis Digital Publishing Pvt Ltd,
2008.

# CHAPTER I

## Due West to Denver

Commencement week at Notre Dame ended in a blaze of glory. Multitudes of guests who had been camping for a night or two in the recitation rooms – our temporary dormitories – gave themselves up to the boyish delights of school-life, and set numerous examples which the students were only too glad to follow. The boat race on the lake was a picture; the champion baseball match, a companion piece; but the highly decorated prize scholars, glittering with gold and silver medals, and badges of satin and bullion; the bevies of beautiful girls who for once – once only in the year – were given the liberty of the lawns, the campus, and the winding forest ways, that make of Notre Dame an elysium in summer; the frequent and inspiring blasts of the University Band, and the general joy that filled every heart to overflowing, rendered the last day of the scholastic year romantic to a degree and memorable forever.

There was no sleep during the closing night – not one solitary wink; all laws were dead-letters – alas that they should so soon arise again from the dead! – and when the wreath of stars that crowns the golden statue of Our Lady on the high dome, two hundred feet in air, and the wide-sweeping crescent under her shining feet, burst suddenly into flame, and shed a lustre that was welcomed for miles and miles over the plains of Indiana – then, I assure you, we were all so deeply touched that we knew not whether to laugh or to weep, and I shall not tell you which we did. The moon was very full that night, and I didn't blame it!

But the picnic really began at the foot of the great stairway in front of the dear old University next morning. Five hundred possible presidents were to be distributed broadcast over the continent; five hundred sons and heirs to be returned with thanks to the yearning bosoms of their respective families. The floodgates of the trunk-rooms were thrown open, and a stream of Saratogas went thundering to the station at South Bend, two miles away. Hour after hour, and indeed for several days, huge trucks and express wagons plied to and fro, groaning under the burden of well-checked luggage. It is astonishing to behold how big a trunk a mere boy may claim for his very own; but it must be remembered that your schoolboy lives for several years within the brass-bound confines of a Saratoga. It is his bureau, his wardrobe, his private library, his museum and toy shop, the receptacle of all that is near and dear to him; it is, in brief, his *sanctum sanctorum*, the one inviolate spot in his whole scholastic career of which he, and he alone, holds the key.

We came down with the tide in the rear of the trunk freshet. The way being more or less clear, navigation was declared open. The next moment saw a procession of chariots, semi-circus wagons and barouches filled with homeward-bound schoolboys and their escorts, dashing at a brisk trot toward the railroad station. Banners were flying, shouts rent the air; familiar forms in cassock and biretta waved benedictions from all points of the compass; while the gladness and the sadness of the hour were perpetuated by the aid of instantaneous photography. The enterprising kodaker caught us on the fly, just as the special train was leaving South Bend for Chicago; a train that was not to be dismembered or its exclusiveness violated until it had been run into the station at Denver.

After this last negative attack we were set free. Vacation had begun in good earnest. What followed, think you? Mutual congratulations, flirtations and fumigations without ceasing; for there was much lost time to be made up, and here was a golden opportunity. O you who have been a schoolboy and lived for months and months in a pent-up Utica, where the glimpse of a girl is as welcome and as rare as a sunbeam in a cellar, you can imagine how the two hours and forty-five minutes were improved – and Chicago eighty miles away. It is true we all turned for a moment to catch a last glimpse of the University dome, towering over the treetops; and we felt very tenderly toward everyone there. But there were "sweet girl graduates" on board; and, as you know well enough, it required no laureate to sing their praises, though he has done so with all the gush and fervor of youth.

It was summer. "It is always summer where they are," some youngster was heard to murmur. But it was really the summer solstice, or very near it. The pond-lilies were ripe; bushels of them were heaped upon the platforms at every station we came to; and before the first stage of our journey was far advanced the girls were sighing over lapfuls of lilies, and the lads tottering under the weight of stupendous *boutonnières*.

As we drew near the Lake City, the excitement visibly increased. Here, there were partings, and such sweet sorrow as poets love to sing. It were vain to tell how many promises were then and there made, and of course destined to be broken; how everybody was to go and spend a happy season with everybody or at least somebody else, and to write meanwhile without fail. There were good-byes again and again, and yet again; and, with much mingled emotion, we settled ourselves in luxurious seats and began to look dreamily toward Denver.

In the mazes of the wonderful city of Chicago we saw the warp of that endless steel web over which we flew like spiders possessed. The sunken switches took our eye and held it for a time. But a greater marvel was the man with the cool head and the keen sight and nerves of iron, who sat up in his loft, with his hand on a magic wand, and played with trainfuls of his fellowmen – a mere question of life or death to be answered over and over again; played with them as the conjurer tosses his handful of pretty globes into the air and catches them without one click of the ivories. It was a forcible reminder of Clapham Junction; the perfect system that brings order out of chaos, and saves a little world, but a mad one, from the total annihilation that threatens it every moment in the hour, and every hour in the day, and every day in the year.

It did not take us long to discover the advantages of our special-car system. There were nigh fifty of us housed in a brace of excursion cars. In one of these

6

– the parlor – the only stationary seats were at the two ends, while the whole floor was covered with easy-chairs of every conceivable pattern. The dining car was in reality a cardroom between meals – and *such* meals, for we had stocked the larder ourselves. Everywhere the agents of the several lines made their appearance and greeted us cordially; they were closeted for a few moments with the shepherd of our flock, Father Zahm, of the University of Notre Dame, Indiana; then they would take a bite with us – a dish of berries or an ice, – for they invariably accompanied us down the road a few miles; and at last would bid us farewell with a flattering figure of speech, which is infinitely preferable to the traditional "Tickets, please; tickets!"

At every town and village crowds came down to see us. We were evidently objects of interest. Even the nimble reporter was on hand, and looked with a not unkindly eye upon the lads who were celebrating the first hours of the vacation with an enthusiasm which had been generating for some weeks. There was such a making up of beds when, at dark, the parlor and dining cars were transformed into long, narrow dormitories, and the boys paired off, two and two, above and below, through the length of our flying university, and made a night of it, without fear of notes or detentions, and with no prefect stalking ghostlike in their midst.

It would be hard to say which we found most diverting, the long, long landscape that divided as we passed, through it and closed up in the rear, leaving only the shining iron seam down the middle; the beautiful, undulating prairie land; the hot and dusty desolation of the plains; the delicious temperature of the highlands, as we approached the Rockies and had our first glimpse of Pike's Peak in its mantle of snow: the muddy rivers, along whose shores we glided swiftly hour after hour: the Mississippi by moonlight – we all sat up to see that – or the Missouri at Kansas City, where we began to scatter our brood among their far Western homes. At La Junta we said good-bye to the boys bound for Mexico and the Southwest. It was like a second closing of the scholastic year; the good-byes were now ringing fast and furious.

Jolly fellows began to grow grave and the serious ones more solemn; for there had been no cloud or shadow for three rollicking days.

To be sure there was a kind of infantile cyclone out on the plains, memorable for its superb atmospheric effects, and the rapidity with which we shut down the windows to keep from being inflated balloon-fashion. And there was a brisk hail-storm at the gate of the Rockies that peppered us smartly for a few moments. Then there were some boys who could not eat enough, and who turned from the dessert in tearful dismay; and one little kid who dived out of the top bunk in a moment of rapture, and should have broken his neck – but he didn't!

We were quite sybaritical as to hours, with breakfast and dinner courses, and mouth-organs and cigarettes and jam between meals. Frosted cake and oranges were left untouched upon the field after the gastronomical battles were fought so bravely three or four times a day. Perhaps the pineapples and bananas, and the open barrel of strawberries, within reach of all at any hour, may account for the phenomenon.

Pueblo! Ah me, the heat of that infernal junction! Pueblo, with the stump of its one memorable tree, or a slice of that stump turned up on end – to make room for a new railway-station, that could just as well have been built a few feet farther on, – and staring at you, with a full broadside of patent-medicine placards trying to cover its nakedness. On closer inspection we read this legend: "The tree that grew here was 380 years old; circumference, 28 feet; height, 79 feet; was cut down June 25, 1883, at a cost of $250." So perished, at the hands of an amazingly stupid city council, the oldest landmark in Colorado. Under the shade of this cottonwood Kit Carson, Wild Bill, and many another famous Indian scout built early camp fires. Near it, in 1850, thirty-six whites were massacred by Indians; upon one of its huge limbs fourteen men were hanged at convenient intervals; and it is a pity that the city council did not follow this admirable lead and leave the one glory of Pueblo to save it from damnation. It afforded the only grateful shelter in this furnace heat; it was the one beautiful object in a most unbeautiful place, and it has been razed to the ground in memory of the block-heads whose bodies were not worthy to enrich the roots of it. Tradition adds, pathetically enough, that the grave of the first white woman who died in that desert was made beneath the boughs of the "Old Monarch." May she rest in peace under the merciless hands of the baggage-master and his merry crew! Lightly lie the trunks that are heaped over her nameless dust! Well, there came a time when we forgot Pueblo, but we never will forgive the town council.

Then we listened in vain at evening for the strumming of fandango music on multitudinous guitars, as was our custom so long as the *muchachos* were with us. Then we played no more progressive euchre games many miles in length, and smoked no more together in the ecstasy of unrestraint; but watched and waited in vain – for those who were with us were no longer of us for some weeks to come, and the mouths of the singers were hushed. The next thing we knew a city seemed to spring suddenly out of the plains – a mirage of brick and mortar – an oasis in the wilderness, – and we realized, with a gasp, that we had struck the bull's-eye of the Far West – in other words, Denver!

# CHAPTER II

## In Denver Town

Colorado! What an open-air sound that word has! The music of the wind is in it, and a peculiarly free, rhythmical swing, suggestive of the swirling lariat. Colorado is not, as some conjecture, a corruption or revised edition of Francisco Vasquez de Coronado, who was sent out by the Spanish Viceroy of Mexico in 1540 in search of the seven cities of Cibola: it is from the verb *colorar* – colored red, or ruddy – a name frequently given to rivers, rocks, and ravines in the lower country. Nor do we care to go back as far as the sixteenth century for the beginning of an enterprise that is still very young and possibly a little fresh. In 1803 the United States purchased from France a vast territory for $15,000,000; it was then known as Louisiana, and that purchase included the district long referred to as the Great American Desert.

In 1806 Zebulon Pike camped where Pueblo now stands. He was a pedestrian.

One day he started to climb a peak whose shining summit had dazzled him from the first; it seemed to soar into the very heavens, yet lie within easy reach just over the neighboring hill. He started bright and early, with enthusiasm in his heart, determination in his eye, and a cold bite in his pocket. He went from hill to hill, from mountain to mountain; always ascending, satisfied that each height was the last, and that he had but to step from the next pinnacle to the throne of his ambition. Alas! the peak was as far away as ever, even at the close of the second day; so famished, foot-frozen and well-nigh in extremity, he dragged his weary bones back to camp, defeated. That peak bears his name to this day, and probably he deserves the honor quite as much as any human molecule who godfathers a mountain.

James Pursley, of Bardstown, Ky., was a greater explorer than Pike; but Pursley gives Pike much credit which Pike blushingly declines. The two men were exceptionally well-bred pioneers. In 1820 Colonel Long named a peak in memory of his explorations. The peak survives. Then came General Fremont, in 1843, and the discovery of gold near Denver fifteen years later; but I believe Green Russell, a Georgian, found *color* earlier on Pike's Peak.

Colorado was the outgrowth of the great financial crisis of 1857. That panic sent a wave westward, – a wave that overflowed all the wild lands of the wilderness, and, in most cases, to the advantage of both wave and wilderness. Of course there was a gradual settling up or settling down from that period. Many people who didn't exactly come to stay got stuck fast, or found it difficult to leave; and now they are glad of it. Denver was the result.

Denver! It seems as if that should be the name of some out-of-door production; of something brawny and breezy and bounding; something strong with the strength of youth; overflowing with vitality; ambitions, unconquerable, irrepressible – and such is Denver, the queen city of the plains. Denver is a marvel, and she knows it. She is by no means the marvel that San Francisco was at the same interesting age; but, then, Denver doesn't know it; or, if she knows it, she doesn't care to mention it or to hear it mentioned.

True it is that the Argonauts of the Pacific were blown in out of the blue sea – most of them. They had had a taste of the tropics on the way; paroquets and Panama fevers were their portion; or, after a long pull and a strong pull around the Horn, they were comparatively fresh and eager for the fray when they touched dry land once more. There was much close company between decks to cheer the lonely hours; a very bracing air and a very broad, bright land to give them welcome when the voyage was ended – in brief, they had their advantages.

The pioneers of Denver town were the captains or mates of prairie schooners, stranded in the midst of a sealike desert. It was a voyage of from six to eight weeks west of the Mississippi in those days. The only stations – and miserably primitive ones at that – lay along Ben Holliday's overland stage route. They were far between. Indians waylaid the voyagers; fires, famine and fatigue helped to strew the trail with the graves of men and the carcasses of animals. Hard lines were these; but not so hard as the lines of those who pushed farther into the wilderness, nor stayed their adventurous feet till they were planted on the rich soil of the Pacific slope.

Pioneer life knows little variety. The *menu* of the Colorado banquet July 4, 1859, will revive in the minds of many an old Californian the fast-fading memories of the past; but I fear, twill be a long time before such a *menu* as the following will gladden the eyes of the average prospector in the Klondyke:

MENU.

SOUP.
A la Bean.

FISH.
Brook Trout, a la catch 'em first.

MEATS.
Antelope larded, pioneer style.

BREAD.
Biscuit, hand-made, full weight, a la

yellow.

## VEGETABLES.
Beans, mountain style, warranted boiled forty-eight hours, a la soda.

## DESSERT.
Dried Apples, Russell gulch style.
Coffee, served in tin cups, to be washed clean for the occasion, overland style, a la no cream.

In those days Horace Greeley, returning from his California tour, halted to cast his eye over the now West. The miners primed an old blunderbus with rich dust, and judiciously salted Gregory gulch. Of course Horace was invited to inspect it. Being somewhat horny-handed, he seized pick and shovel and went to work in earnest. The pan-out was astonishing. He flew back to New York laden with the glittering proofs of wealth; gave a whole page of the *Tribune* to his tale of the golden fleece; and a rush to the new diggings followed as a matter of course.

Denver and Auraria were rival settlements on the opposite shores of Cherry Creek; in 1860 they consolidated, and then boasted a population of 4000, in a vast territory containing but 60,000 souls. The boom was on, and it was not long before a parson made his appearance. This was the Rev. George Washington Fisher of the Methodist Church, who accepted the offer of a saloon as a house of worship, using the bar for a pulpit. His text was: "Ho, everyone that thirsteth! come ye to the waters. And he that hath no money, come ye, buy and eat. Yea, come buy wine and milk without money and without price." On the walls were displayed these legends: "No trust," "Pay as you go," "Twenty-five cents a drink," etc.

Colorado Territory was organized in 1861, and was loyal to the Union. Denver was still booming, though she suffered nearly all the ills that precocious settlements are heir to. The business portion of the town was half destroyed in 1863; Cherry Creek flooded her in 1864, floating houses out of reach and drowning fifteen or twenty of the inhabitants. Then the Indians went on the war-path; stages and wagon trains were attacked; passengers and scattered settlers massacred, and the very town itself threatened. Alarm-bells warned the frightened inhabitants of impending danger; many fled to the United States Mint for refuge, and to cellars, cisterns, and dark alleys. This was during the wild reign of Spotted Horse along the shores of the Platte, before he was captured by Major Downing at the battle of Sand Creek, and finally sent to Europe on exhibition as a genuine child of the forest.

Those were stirring times, when every man had an eye to business, and could hardly afford to spare it long enough to wink. It is related of a certain minister who was officiating at a funeral that, while standing by the coffin offering the final prayer, he noticed one of the mourners kneeling upon the loose earth recently thrown from the grave. This man was a prospector, like all the rest, and in an absent-minded way he had tearfully been sifting the soil through his fingers. Suddenly he arose and began to stake out a claim adjoining the grave. This was, of course, observed by the clergyman, who hastened the ceremonials to a conclusion, and ended his prayer thus: "Stake me off a claim, Bill. We ask it for Christ's sake. Amen."

Horace Greeley's visit was fully appreciated, and his name given to a mountain hamlet, long after known familiarly as "Saint's Rest," because there was nothing stimulating to be found thereabout. Poor Meeker, for many years agricultural editor of the New York *Tribune*, founded that settlement. He was backed by Greeley, and established the Greeley *Tribune* at Saint's Rest. In 1877 Meeker was made Indian agent, and he did his best to live up to the dream of the Indian-maniacs; but, after two years of self-sacrifice and devotion to the cause, he was brutally betrayed and murdered by Chief Douglas, of the Utes, his guest at the time. Mrs. Meeker and her daughters, and a Mrs. Price and her child, were taken captive and subjected to the usual treatment which all women and children may expect at the hands of the noble red-man. They were rescued in due season; but what was rescue to them save a prolongation of inconsolable bereavement?

When General Grant visited Central, the little mountain town received him royally. A pavement of solid silver bricks was laid for him to walk upon from his carriage to the hotel door. One sees very little of this barbaric splendor nowadays even in Denver, the most pretentious of far Western burgs. She is a metropolis of magnificent promises. Alighting at the airy station, you take a carriage for the hotel, and come at once to the centre of the city. Were you to continue your drive but a few blocks farther, you would come with equal abruptness to the edge of it. The surprise is delightful in either case, but the suddenness of the transition makes the stranger guest a little dizzy at first. There are handsome buildings in Denver – blocks that would do credit to any city under the sun; but there was for years an upstart air, a palpable provincialism, a kind of ill-disguised "previousness," noticeable that made her seem like the brisk suburb of some other place, and that other place, alas! invisible to mortal eye. Rectangular blocks make a checker-board of the town map. The streets are appropriately named Antelope, Bear, Bison, Boulder, Buffalo, Coyote, Cedar, Cottonwood, Deer, Golden, Granite, Moose, etc. The names of most trees, most precious stones, the great States and Territories of the West, with a sprinkling of Spanish, likewise beguile you off into space, and leave the once nebulous burg beaming in the rear.

Denver's theatre is remarkably handsome. In hot weather the atmosphere is tempered by torrents of ice-water that crash through hidden aqueducts with a sound as of twenty sawmills. The management *dams* the flood when the curtain rises and the players begin to speak; the music lovers *damn* it from the moment the curtain falls. They are absorbed in volumes of silent profanity between the acts; for the orchestra is literally drowned in the roar of the rushing element. There was nothing that interested me more than a copy of Alice Polk Hill's "Tales of the Colorado Pioneers"; and to her I return thanks for all that I borrowed without leave from that diverting volume.

Somehow Denver, after my early visit, leaves with me an impression as of a perfectly new city that has just been unpacked; as if the various parts of it had been set up in a great hurry, and the citizens were now impatiently awaiting the arrival of the rest of the properties. Some of the streets that appeared so well at first glance, seemed, upon inspection, more like theatrical flats than realities; and there was always a consciousness of everything being wide open and uncovered. Indeed, so strongly did I feel this that it was with difficulty I could refrain from wearing my hat in the house. Nor could I persuade myself that it was quite safe to go out alone after dark, lest unwittingly I should get lost, and lift up in vain the voice of one crying in the wilderness; for the blank and weird spaces about there are as wide as the horizon where the distant mountains seem to have slid partly down the terrestrial incline, – spaces that offer the unwary neither hope nor hospice, – where there is positively shelter for neither man nor beast, from the red-brick heart of the ambitious young city to her snow-capped ultimate suburb.

# CHAPTER III

## The Garden of the Gods

The trains run out of Denver like quick-silver, – this is the prettiest thing I can say of Denver. They trickle down into high, green valleys, under the shadow of snow-capped cliffs. There the grass is of the liveliest tint – a kind of salad-green. The air is sweet and fine; everything looks clean, well kept, well swept – perhaps the wind is the keeper and the sweeper. All along the way there is a very striking contrast of color in rock, meadows, and sky; the whole is as appetizing to the sight as a newly varnished picture.

We didn't down brakes until we reached Colorado Springs; there we changed cars for Manitou. Already the castellated rocks were filling us with childish delight. Fungi decked the cliffs above us: colossal, petrified fungi, painted Indian fashion. At any rate, there is a kind of wild, out-of-door, subdued harmony in the rock-tints upon the exterior slopes of the famed Garden of the Gods, quite in keeping with the spirit of the decorative red-man. Within that garden color and form run riot, and Manitou is the restful outpost of this erratic wilderness.

It is fitting that Manitou should be approached in a rather primitive manner. I was glad when we were very politely invited to get out of the train and walk a plank over a puddle that for a moment submerged the track; glad when we were advised to foot it over a trestle-bridge that sagged in the swift current of a swollen stream; and gladder still when our locomotive began to puff and blow and slaken its pace as we climbed up into the mouth of a ravine fragrant with the warm scents of summer – albeit we could boast but a solitary brace of cars, and these small ones, and not overcrowded at that.

Only think of it! We were scarcely three hours by rail from Denver; and yet here, in Manitou, were the very elements so noticeably lacking there. Nature in her natural state – primitive forever; the air seasoned with the pungent spices of odoriferous herbs; the sweetest sunshine in abundance, and all the shade that makes sunshine most agreeable.

Manitou is a picturesque hamlet that has scattered itself up and down a deep ravine, regardless of the limiting lines of the surveyor. The railway station at Manitou might pose for a porter's lodge in the prettiest park in England. Surely there is hope for America when she can so far curb her vulgar love of the merely practical as to do that sort of thing at the right time and in the right place.

A fine stream brawls through the bed of this lovely vale. There are rustic cottages that cluster upon the brink of the stream, as if charmed by the music of its song; and I am sure that the cottagers dwelling therein have no wish to hang their harps upon any willows whatever; or to mingle their tears, though these were indeed the waters of Babylon that flow softly night and day through the green groves of Manitou. The breeze stirs the pulse like a tonic; birds, bees, and butterflies dance in the air; the leaves have the gloss of varnish – there is no dust there, – and everything is cleanly, cheerful and reposeful. From the hotel veranda float the strains of harp and viol; at intervals during the day and night music helps us to lift up our hearts; there is nothing like it – except more of it. There is not overmuch dressing among the women, nor the beastly spirit of loudness among the men; the domestic atmosphere is undisturbed. A newspaper printed on a hand-press, and distributed by the winds for aught I know, has its office in the main lane of the village; its society column creates no scandal. A solitary bicycle that flashes like a shooting star across the placid foreground is our nearest approach to an event worth mentioning.

Loungers lounge at the springs as if they really enjoyed it. An amiable booth-boy displays his well-dressed and handsomely mounted foxskins, his pressed flowers of Colorado, his queer mineralogical jewelry, and his uncouth geological specimens in the shape of hideous bric-a-brac, as if he took pleasure in thus entertaining the public; while everybody has the cosiest and most sociable time over the counter, and buys only by accident at last.

There are rock gorges in Manitou, through which the Indian tribes were wont noiselessly to defile when on the war-path in the brave days of old; gorges where currents of hot air breathe in your face like the breath of some fierce animal. There are brilliant and noisy cataracts and cascades that silver the rocks with spray; and a huge winding cavern filled with mice and filth and the blackness of darkness, and out of which one emerges looking like a tramp and feeling like – well! There are springs bubbling and steeping and stagnating by the wayside; springs containing carbonates of soda, lithia, lime, magnesia, and iron; sulphates of potassa and soda, chloride of sodium and silica, in various solutions. Some of these are sweeter than honey in the honeycomb; some of them smell to heaven – what more can the pampered palate of man desire?

Let all those who thirst for chalybeate waters bear in mind that the Ute Iron Spring of Manitou is 800 feet higher than St. Catarina, the highest iron spring in Europe, and nearly 1000 feet higher than St. Moritz; and that the bracing air at an elevation of 6400 feet has probably as much to do with the recovery of the invalid as has the judicious quaffing of medicinal waters. Of pure iron springs, the famous Schwalbach contains rather more iron than the Ute Iron, and Spa rather less. On the whole, Manitou has the advantage of the most celebrated medicinal springs in Europe, and has a climate even in midwinter preferable to all of them.

On the edge of the pretty hamlet at Manitou stands a cottage half hidden like a bird's nest among the trees. I saw only the peaks of gables under green boughs; and I wondered when I was informed that the lovely spot had been long untenanted, and wondered still more when I learned that it was the property of good Grace Greenwood. Will she ever cease wandering, and return to weave a new chaplet of greenwood leaves gathered beneath the eaves of her mountain home?

At the top of the village street stands Pike's Peak – at least it seems to stand there when viewed through the telescopic air. It is in reality a dozen miles distant; but is easily approached by a winding trail, over which ladies in the saddle may reach the glorious snow-capped summit and return to Manitou between breakfast and supper – unless one should prefer to be rushed up and down over the aerial railway. From the signal station the view reminds one of a map of the world. It rather dazes than delights the eye to roam so far, and imagination itself grows weary at last and is glad to fold its wings.

Manitou's chief attraction lies over the first range of hills – the veritable Garden of the Gods. You may walk, ride or drive to it; in any case the surprise begins the moment you reach the ridge's top above Manitou, and ceases not till the back is turned at the close of the excursion – nor then either, for the memory of that marvel haunts one like a feverish dream. Fancy a softly undulating land, delicately wooded and decked with many an ornamental shrub; a landscape that composes so well one can scarcely assure himself that the artist or the landscape gardener has not had a hand in the beautifying of it.

In this lonely, silent land, with cloud shadows floating across it, at long intervals bird voices or the bleating of distant flocks charm the listening ear. Out of this wild and beautiful spot spring Cyclopean rocks, appalling in the splendor of their proportions and the magnificence of their dyes. Sharp shafts shoot heavenward from breadths of level sward, and glow like living flames; peaks of various tinges overlook the tops of other peaks, that, in their turn, lord it among gigantic bowlders piled upon massive pedestals. It is Ossa upon Pelion, in little; vastly impressive because of the exceptional surroundings that magnify these magnificent monuments, unique in their design and almost unparalleled in their picturesque and daring outline. Some of the monoliths tremble and sway, or seem to sway; for they are balanced edgewise, as if the gods had amused themselves in some infantile game, and, growing weary of this little planet, had fled and left their toys in confusion. The top-heavy and the tottering ones are almost within reach; but there are slabs of rock that look like slices out of a mountain –

I had almost said like slices out of a red-hot volcano; they stand up against the blue sky and the widespreading background in brilliant and astonishing perspective.

I doubt if anywhere else in the world the contrasts in color and form are more violent than in the Garden of the Gods. They are not always agreeable to the eye, for there is much crude color here; but there are points of sight where these columns, pinnacles, spires and obelisks, with base and capital, are so grouped that the massing is as fantastical as a cloud picture, and the whole can be compared only to a petrified after-glow. I have seen pictures of the Garden of the Gods that made me nearly burst with laughter; I mean color studies that were supremely ridiculous in my eyes, for I had not then seen the original; but none of these makes me laugh any longer. They serve, even the wildest and the worst of them, to remind me of a morning drive, in the best of company, through that grand garden where our combined vocabularies of delight and wonderment were exhausted inside of fifteen minutes; and where we drove on and on, hour after hour, from climax to climax, lost in speechless amazement.

Glen Eyrie is the valley of Rasselas – I am sure it is. The Prince of Abyssinia left the gate open when he, poor fool! went forth in search of happiness and found it not. Now any one may drive through the domain of the present possessor and admire his wealth of pictorial solitude – without, however, sharing it further. If it were mine, would I permit thus much, I wonder? Only the elect should enter there; and once the charmed circle was complete, we would wall up the narrow passage that leads to this terrestrial paradise, and you would hear no more from us, or of us, nor we of you, or from you, forever.

On my first visit to Colorado Springs I made a little pilgrimage. I heard that a gentle lady, whom I had always wished to see, was at her home on the edge of the city. No trouble in finding the place: any one could direct me. It was a cosy cottage in the midst of a garden and shaded by thickly leaved trees. Some one was bowed down among the strawberry beds, busy there; yet the place seemed half deserted and very, very quiet. Big bamboo chairs and lounges lined the vine-curtained porch. The shades in the low bay-window were half drawn, and a glint of sunshine lighted the warm interior. I saw heaps of precious books on the table in that deep window. There was a mosquito door in the porch, and there I knocked for admittance. I knocked for a long time, but received no answer. I knocked again so that I might be heard even in the strawberry bed. A little kitten came up out of the garden and said something kittenish to me, and then I heard a muffled step within. The door opened – the inner door, – and beyond the wire-cloth screen, that remained closed against me, I saw a figure like a ghost, but a very buxom and wholesome ghost indeed.

I asked for the hostess. Alas! she was far away and had been ill; it was not known when she would return. Her address was offered me, and I thought to write her, – thought to tell her how I had sought out her home, hoping to find her after years of patient waiting; and that while I talked of her through the wire-cloth screen the kitten, which she must have petted once upon a time, climbed up the screen until it had reached the face of the amiable woman within, and then purred and purred as only a real kitten can. I never wrote that letter; for while we were chatting on the porch she of whom we chatted, she who has written a whole armful of the most womanly and lovable of books, Helen Hunt Jackson, lay dying in San Francisco and we knew it not. But it is something to have stood by her threshold, though she was never again to cross it in the flesh, and to have been greeted by her kitten. How she loved kittens! And now I can associate her memory with the peacefulest of cottages, the easiest of veranda chairs, a bay-window full of books and sunshine, and a strawberry bed alive with berries and blossoms and butterflies and bees. And yonder on the heights her body was anon laid to rest among the haunts she loved so dearly.

# CHAPTER IV

# A Whirl across the Rockies

A long time ago – nearly a quarter of a century – California could boast a literary weekly capable of holding its own with any in the land. This was before San Francisco had begun to lose her unique and delightful individuality – now gone forever. Among the contributors to this once famous weekly were Mark Twain, Bret Harte, Prentice Mulford, Joaquin Miller, Dan de Quille, Orpheus C. Kerr, C. H. Webb, "John Paul," Ada Clare, Ada Isaacs Menken, Ina Coolbrith, and hosts of others. Fitz Hugh Ludlow wrote for it a series of brilliant descriptive letters recounting his adventures during a recent overland journey; they were afterward incorporated in a volume – long out of print – entitled "The Heart of the Continent."

In one of these letters Ludlow wrote as follows of the probable future of Manitou: "When Colorado becomes a populous State, the springs of the

Fontaine-qui-Bouille will constitute its Spa. In air and scenery no more glorious summer residence could be imagined. The Coloradian of the future, astonishing the echoes of the rocky foothills by a railroad from Denver to the springs, and running down on Saturday to stop over Sunday with his family, will have little cause to envy us Easterners our Saratoga as he paces up and down the piazza of the Spa hotel, mingling his full-flavored Havana with that lovely air, unbreathed before, which is floating down upon him from the snow peaks of the range." His prophecy has become true in every particular. But what would he have thought had he threaded the tortuous path now marked by glistening railway tracks? What would he have said of the Grand Cañon of the Arkansas, the Black Cañon of the Gunnison, Castle Cañon and Marshall Pass over the crest of the continent?

I suppose a narrow-gauge road can go anywhere. It trails along the slope of shelving hills like a wild vine; it slides through gopher-hole tunnels as a thread slides through the eye of a needle; it utilizes water-courses; it turns ridiculously sharp corners in a style calculated to remind one of the days when he played "snap-the-whip" and happened to be the snapper himself. This is especially the case if one is sitting on the rear platform of the last car. We shot a cañon by daylight, and marvelled at the glazed surface of the red rock with never so much as a scratch over it. On the one hand we nearly scraped the abrupt perpendicular wall that towered hundreds of feet above us; on the other, a swift, muddy torrent sprang at our stone-bedded sleepers as if to snatch them away; while it flooded the cañon to the opposite wall, that did not seem more that a few yards distant. The stream was swollen, and went howling down the ravine full of sound and fury – which in this case, however, signified a good deal.

Once we stopped and took an observation, for the track was under water; then we waded cautiously to the mainland, across the sunken section, and thanked our stars that we were not boycotted by the elements at that inhospitable point. Once we paused for a few minutes to contemplate the total wreck of a palace car that had recently struck a projecting bowlder – and spattered.

The camps along the track are just such as may be looked for in the waste places of the earth – temporary shelter for wayfarers whose homes are under their hats. The thin stream of civilization that trickles off into the wilderness, following the iron track, makes puddles now and again. Some of these dwindle away soon enough – or perhaps not quite soon enough; some of them increase and become permanent and beautiful.

Night found us in the Black Cañon of the Gunnison. Could any time be more appropriate? Clouds rolled over us in dense masses, and at intervals the moon flashed upon us like a dark lantern. Could anything be more picturesque? We knew that much of the darkness, the blackness of darkness, was adamantine rock; some of it an inky flood – a veritable river of death – rolling close beneath us, but quite invisible most of the time; and the night itself a profound mystery, through which we burned an endless tunnel – like a firebrand hurled into space.

Now and again the heavens opened, and then we saw the moon soaring among the monumental peaks; but the heights were so cloudlike and the cloud masses so solid we could not for the life of us be certain of the nature of either. There were cañons like huge quarries, and cañons like rocky mazes, where we seemed to have rushed headlong into a *cul de sac*, and were in danger of dashing our brains out against the mighty walls that loomed before us. There was many a winding stream which we took at a single bound, and occasionally an oasis, green and flowery; but, oh, so few habitations and so few spots that one would really care to inhabit!

Marshall Pass does very well for once; it is an experience and a novelty – what else is there in life to make it livable save a new experience or the hope of one? Such a getting up hill as precedes the rest at the summit! We stopped for breath while the locomotive puffed and panted as if it would burst its brass-bound lungs; then we began to climb again, and to wheeze, fret and fume; and it seemed as if we actually went down on hands and knees and crept a bit when the grade became steeper than usual. Only think of it a moment – an incline of two hundred and twenty feet to the mile in some places, and the track climbing over itself at frequent intervals. Far below us we saw the terraces we had passed long before; far above us lay the great land we were so slowly and so painfully approaching. At last we reached the summit, ten thousand eight hundred and twenty feet above sea level – a God-forsaken district, bristling with dead trees, and with hardly air enough to go around.

We stopped in a long shed – built to keep off the sky, I suppose. Gallants prospected for flowers and grass-blades, and received the profuse thanks of the fair in exchange for them. Then we glided down into the snow lands that lay beyond – filled with a delicious sense of relief, for a fellow never feels so mean or so small a pigmy as when perched on an

Alpine height.

More cañons followed, and no two alike; then came plain after plain, with buttes outlined in the distance; more plains, with nothing but their own excessive plainness to boast of. We soon grew vastly weary; for most plains are, after all, mere platitudes. And then Salt Lake City, the Mormon capital, with its lake shimmering like a mirage in the great glow of the valley; and a run due north through the well-tilled lands of the thrifty "saints," getting our best wayside meals at stations where buxom Mormon women served us heartily; still north and west, flying night and day out of the insufferable summer dust that makes ovens of those midland valleys. There was a rich, bracing air far north, and grand forests of spicy pine, and such a Columbia river-shore to follow as is worth a week's travel merely to get one glimpse of; and at last Portland, the prettiest of Pacific cities, and heaps of friends to greet me there.

Bright days were to follow, as you shall soon see; for I was still bound northward, with no will to rest until I had plowed the floating fields of ice and dozed through the pale hours of an arctic summer under the midnight sun.

# CHAPTER V

## Off for Alaska

If you are bound for Alaska, you can make the round trip most conveniently and comfortably by taking the steamer at Portland, Oregon, and retaining your state-room until you land again in Portland, three weeks later. Or you can run north by rail as far as Tacoma; there board a fine little steamer and skim through the winding water-ways of Puget Sound (as lovely a sheet of water as ever the sun shone on), debark at Port Townsend, and here await the arrival of the Alaska steamer, which makes its excursion trip monthly – at least it used to before the Klondyke hoards deranged the time-table and the times.

If this does not satisfy you, you may take passage at San Francisco for Port Townsend or Victoria, and connect at either port with the Alaska boat. Those who are still unsuited had better wait a bit, when, no doubt, other as entirely satisfactory arrangements will be made for their especial convenience. I went by train to Tacoma. I wanted to sniff the forest scents of Washington State, and to get a glimpse of the brave young settlements scattered through the North-western wilderness. I wanted to skirt the shore of the great Sounds, whose praises have been ringing in my ears ever since I can remember – and that is a pretty long time now.

I wanted to loaf for a while in Port Townsend, the old jumping-off place, the monogram in the extreme northwest corner of the map of the United States of America – at least such it was until the Alaskan annex stretched the thing all out of shape, and planted our flag so far out in the Pacific that San Francisco lies a little east of the centre of the Union, and the Hawaiian islands come within our boundaries; for our Aleutian-island arm, you know, stretches a thousand miles to the west of Hawaii – it even chucks Asia under the chin.

But now let me offer you a stray handful of leaves from my note-book – mere suggestions of travel.

At Portland took morning train for Tacoma, one hundred and forty-seven miles. Swarms of people at the station, and some ominous "good-byes"; the majority talking of Alaska in a superior fashion, which implies that they are through passengers, and they don't care who knows it. Alaska boat left Portland two days ago; we are to catch her at Port Townsend, and it looks as if we should crowd her. Train crosses the Columbia River on a monster ferry; a jolly and restful half hour in the cars and out of them.

A very hot and dusty ride through Washington State, – part of it pretty enough and part of it by no means so. Cars full of screaming babies, sweltering tourists, and falling cinders that sting like dumb mosquitoes. Rather a mixed neighborhood on the rail. An effusively amiable evangelist bobs up almost immediately, – one of those fellows whom no amount of snubbing can keep under. Old Probabilities is also on board, discoursing at intervals to all who will give ear. Some quiet and interesting folk in a state of suspense, and one young fellow – a regular trump,

– promise better things.

We reach Tacoma at 6.30 p. m.; a queer, scattering town on Commencement Bay, at the head of Puget Sound. Very deep water just off shore. Two boys in a sailboat are blown about at the mercy of the fitful wind; boat on beam-ends; boys on the uppermost gunwale; sail lying flat on the water. But nobody seems to care, not even the young castaways. Perhaps the inhabitants of Tacoma are amphibious. Very beautiful sheet of water, this Puget Sound; long, winding, monotonous shores; trees all alike, straight up and down, mostly pines and cedars; shores rather low, and outline too regular for much picturesque effect. Tacoma commands the best view of the Sound and of Mt. Tacoma, with its fifteen thousand perpendicular feet looming rose-pink in the heavens, and all its fifteen glaciers seeming to glow with an inner tropic warmth. There are eighteen hundred miles of shore-line embroidering this marvellous Sound. We are continually rounding abrupt points, as in a river, – points so much alike that an untutored eye can not tell one from another. Old Probabilities industriously taking his reckonings and growing more and more enthusiastic at every turn – especially so when the after-glow burns the sea to a coal; it reminds him of a volcanic eruption. There are some people who when they see anything new to them are instantly reminded of something else they have seen, and the new object becomes second rate on the spot. A little travel is a dangerous thing.

Pay $3.25 for my fare from Tacoma to Port Townsend, and find a moment later that some are paying only $1 for the same accommodations. Competition is the mother of these pleasant surprises, but it is worth thrice the original price – the enjoyment of this twilight cruise. More after-glow, much more, with the Olympian Mountains lying between us and the ocean. In the foreground is a golden flood with scarlet ripples breaking through it – a vision splendid and long continued. Air growing quite chilly; strong draughts at some of the turns in the stream. Surely, in this case, the evening and the morning are not the same day.

At 9.30 p. m. we approach Seattle – a

handsome town, with its terraces of lights twinkling in the gloaming. Passengers soon distribute themselves through the darkness. I am left alone on the after-deck to watch the big, shadowy ships that are moored near us, and the exquisite phosphorescent light in the water – a wave of ink with the luminous trail of a struck match smouldering across it. Far into the night there was the thundering of freight rolling up and down the decks, and the ring of invisible truck-wheels.

Slept by and by, and was awakened by the prolonged shriek of a steam whistle and a stream of sunlight that poured in at my state-room window. We were backing and slowing off Port Ludlow. Big sawmill close at hand. Four barks lie at the dock in front of it; a few houses stand on the hill above; pine woods crowd to the water's edge, making the place look solemn. Surely it is a solemn land and a solemn sea about here. After breakfast, about 8.30 o'clock, Port Townsend hove in sight, and here we await the arrival of the Alaska boat. What an odd little town it is – the smallest possible city set upon a hill; the business quarter huddled at the foot of the hill, as if it had slid down there and lodged on the very edge of the sea! The hotels stalk out over the water on stilts. One sleeps well in the sweet salt air, lulled by the murmur of the waves under the veranda.

I rummage the town in search of adventure; climb one hundred and fifty steep steps, and find the highlands at the top, green, pastoral and reposeful. Pleasant homes are scattered about; a few animals feed leisurely in the grassy streets. One diminutive Episcopal chapel comes near to being pretty, yet stops just short of it. But there is a kind of unpretending prettiness in the bright and breezy heights environed by black forest and blue sea.

A revenue cutter – this is a port of customs, please remember – lies in the offing. She looks as if she were suspended in air, so pure are the elements in the northland. I lean from a parapet, on my way down the seaward face of the cliff, and hear the order, "Make ready!" Then comes a flash of flame, a white, leaping cloud, and a crash that shatters an echo into fragments all along the shore; while beautiful smoke rings roll up against the sky like victorious wreaths.

I call on the Hon. J. G. Swan, Hawaiian Consul, author of "The Northwest Coast; or, Three Years' Residence in Washington Territory." Find him delightful, and delightfully situated in a perfect museum of Indian relics; himself full of the liveliest recollections of Indian life, and quite an authority on Indian tongues and traditions; find also an old schoolmate, after long years of separation, and am most courteously entertained. What a drive we had over the hills and along the beach, where the crows haunt the water's edge like sea-birds! It has been repeatedly affirmed that these crows have been seen to seize a clam, raise it high in the air, let it drop upon a rock, and then pounce upon the fragments and feast furiously. But I have never seen one who has had ocular proof of this.

There was a very happy hour spent at Colonel Douglas' quarters, over at the camp; and then such a long, long drive through the deep wildwood, with its dense undergrowth, said to be the haunt of bear, panther, wild cat, deer, and other large game. Bearberries grew in profusion everywhere. The road, kept in splendid repair by the army men, dipped into a meadow full of savage mosquitoes; but escaping through two gates, we struck again into the forest, where the road was almost overgrown with dew-damp brush, that besprinkled us profusely as we passed.

We paused upon the slope above Port Discovery Bay; saw an old fellow on the porch of a wee cottage looking steadfastly into the future – across the Bay; with pipe in mouth, he was the picture of contentment, abstraction and repose. He never once turned to look at us, though few pass that way; but kept his eyes fixed upon a vision of surpassing beauty, where the vivid coloring was startling to the eye and the morning air like an elixir. Nothing but the great summer hotel of the future – it will surely come some day and stand right there – can rob the spot of its blissful serenity.

# CHAPTER VI

## In the Inland Sea

We were waiting the arrival of the Alaska boat, – wandering aimlessly about the little town, looking off upon the quiet sea, now veiled in a dense smoke blown down from the vast forest fires that were sweeping the interior. The sun, shorn of his beams, was a disk of copper; the sun-track in the sea, a trail of blood. The clang of every ship's bell, the scream of every whistle, gave us new hope; but we were still waiting, waiting, waiting. Port Townsend stands knee-deep in the edge of a sea-garden. I sat a long time on the dock, watching for some sign of the belated boat. Great ropes of kelp, tubes of dark brown sea-grass, floated past me on the slow tide. Wonderful anemones, pink, balloon-shaped, mutable, living and breathing things, – these panted as they drifted by. At every respiration they expanded like the sudden blossoming of a flower; then they closed quite as suddenly, and became mere buds. When the round core of these sea-flowers was exposed to the air – the palpitating heart was just beneath the surface most of the time, – they withered in a breath; but revived again the moment the water glazed them over, and fairly revelled in aqueous efflorescence.

"Bang!" It was the crash of an unmistakable gun, that shook the town to its foundations and brought the inhabitants to their feet in an instant. Out of the smoke loomed a shadowy ship, and, lo! it was the Alaska boat. A goodly number of passengers were already on board; as many more were now to join her; and then her prow was to be turned to the north star and held there for some time to come. In a moment the whole port was in a state of excitement. New arrivals hurried on shore to see the lions of the place. We, who had been anxiously awaiting this hour for a couple of long summer days, took the ship by storm, and drove the most amiable and obliging of pursers nearly frantic with our pressing solicitations.

Everybody was laying in private stores, this being our last chance to supply all deficiencies. Light literature we found scattered about at the druggist's and the grocer's and the curiosity shops; also ink, pens, note-books, tobacco, scented soap and playing-cards were discovered in equally unexpected localities. We all wanted volumes on the Northwest – as many of them as we could get; but almost the only one obtainable was Skidmore's "Alaska, the Sitkan Archipelago," which is as good as any, if not the best. A few had copies of the "Pacific Coast Pilot. Alaska. Part I. Dixon's Entrance to Yakutat Bay," – invaluable as a practical guide, and filled with positive data. Dall and Whimper we could not find, nor Bancroft at that time. Who will give us a handy volume reprint of delightful old Vancouver?

We were busy as bees all that afternoon; yet the night and the starlight saw us satisfactorily hived, and it was not long before the buzzing ceased, as ship and shore slept the sleep of the just. By and by we heard pumping, hosing, deck-washing, the paddling of bare feet to and fro, and all the familiar sounds of an early morning at sea. The ship, however, was motionless: we were lying stock-still. Doubtless everybody was wondering at this, as I was, when there came a crash, followed by a small avalanche of broken timber, while the ship quaked in her watery bed. I thought of dynamite and the *Dies Irae*; but almost immediately the cabin-boy, who appeared with the matutinal coffee, said it was only the *Olympian*, the fashionable Sound steamer, that had run into us, as was her custom. She is always running into something, and she succeeded in carrying away a portion of our stern gear on this occasion. Nevertheless, we were delayed only a few hours; for the *Olympian* was polite enough not to strike us below the water-line, and so by high noon we were fairly under way.

From my log-book I take the following: This is slow and easy sailing – a kind of jog-trot over the smoothest possible sea, with the paddles audibly working every foot of the way. We run down among the San Juan Islands, where the passages are so narrow and so intricate they make a kind of watery monogram among the fir-lined shores. A dense smoke still obscures the sun, – a rich haze that softens the distance and lends a picturesqueness that is perhaps not wholly natural to the locality, though the San Juan Islands are unquestionably beautiful.

The Gulf of Georgia, the Straits of Fuca, and Queen Charlotte Sound are the words upon the lips of everybody. Shades of my schoolboy days! How much sweeter they taste here than in the old geography class! Before us stretches a wilderness of islands, mostly uninhabited, which penetrates even into the sunless winter and the shadowless summer of Behring Sea.

As for ourselves, Old Probabilities has got down to business. He has opened an impromptu peripatetic school of navigation, and triumphantly sticks a pin into every point that tallies with his yard-square chart. The evangelist has his field-glass to his eye in search of the unregenerated aborigines. The swell tourists are much swollen with travel; they loosen the belts of their Norfolks, and at intervals affect a languid interest in this mundane sphere. There are delightful people on board – many of them – and not a few others. There are bevies of girls – all young, all pretty; and all, or nearly all, bubbling over with hearty and wholesome laughter.

What richness! A good, clean deck running the whole length of the ship; a cosy and cheerful social hall, with a first-class upright piano of delicious tone, and at least a half dozen creditable performers to awaken the soul of it; a good table, good weather, good luck, and positively nothing to do but have a good time for three solid weeks in the wilderness. The pestiferous telephone can not play the earwig on board this ship; the telegraph, with metallic tick, can not once startle us by precipitating town tattle; the postal service is cut off; wars and rumors of wars, the annihilation of a nation, even the swallowing up of a whole continent, are now of less consequence to us than the possibility of a rain-shower this afternoon, or the solution of the vexed question, "Will the aurora dazzle us before dawn?" We do not propose to wait upon the aurora: for days and days and days we are going to climb up the globe due North, getting nearer and nearer to it all the while. Now, inasmuch as everything is new to us, we can easily content ourselves for hours by lounging in the easy-chairs, and looking off upon the placid sea, and at the perennial verdure that springs out of it and mantles a lovely but lonely land.

Only think of it for a moment! Here on the northwest coast there are islands sown so thickly that many of the sea-passages, though deep enough for a three-decker to swim in, are so narrow that one might easily skim his hat across them. There are thousands of these islands – yea, tens of thousands, – I don't know just how many, and perhaps no man does. They are of all shapes and sizes, and the majority of them are handsomely wooded. The sombre green of the woods, stretching between the sombre blue-green of the water and the opaline sheen of the sky, forms a picture – a momentary picture, – the chief features of which change almost as suddenly and quite as completely as the transformations in a kaleidoscope. We are forever turning corners; and no sooner are we around one corner than three others elbow us just ahead. Now, toward which of the three are we bound, and will our good ship run to larboard or to starboard? This is a turn one might bet on all day long – and lose nearly every time.

A bewildering cruise! Vastly finer than river sailing is this Alaskan expedition. Here is a whole tangle of rivers full of strange tides, mysterious currents, and sweet surprises. Moreover, we can get lost if we want to – no one can get lost in a river. We can rush in where pilots fear to tread, strike sunken rocks, toss among dismal eddies, or plunge into whirlpools. We can rake overhanging boughs with our yard-arms if we want to – but we don't want to. In 1875 the United States steamer *Saranac* went down in Seymour Narrows, and her fate was sudden death. The United States steamer *Suwanee* met with a like misfortune on entering Queen Charlotte Sound. It is rather jolly to think of these things, and to realize that we were in more or less danger; though the shores are as silent as the grave, the sea sleeps like a mill-pond, and the sun sinks to rest with great dignity and precision, nightly bathing the lonely North in sensuous splendor.

It is getting late. Most of us are indulging in a constitutional. We rush up and down the long flush decks like mad; we take fiendish delight in upsetting the pious dignity of the evangelist; we flutter the smokers in the smoking-room – because, forsooth, we are chasing the girls from one end of the ship to the other; and consequently the denizens of the masculine cabin can give their undivided attention to neither cards nor tobacco. What fun it all is – when one is not obliged to do it for a living, and when it is the only healthy exercise one is able to take!

By and by the girls fly to their little nests. As we still stroll in the ever-so-late twilight, at 10 p. m., we hear them piping sleepily, one to another, their heads under their wings no doubt. They are early birds – but that is all right. They are the life of the ship; but for their mirth and music the twilight would be longer and less delightful. Far into the night I linger over a final cigarette. An inexpressible calm steals over me, – a feeling as of deliverance, for the time being at least, from all the cares of this world. We are steaming toward a mass of shadows that, like iron gates, seem shut against us. A group of fellow-voyagers gathers on the forward deck, resolved to sit up and ascertain whether we really manage to squeeze through some crevice, or back out at last and go around the block. I grow drowsy and think fondly of my little bunk.

What a night! Everything has grown vague and mysterious. Not a voice is heard – only the throb of the engine down below and the articulated pulsation of the paddles, every stroke of which brings forth a hollow sound from the sea, as clear and as well defined as a blow upon a drumhead; but these are softened by the swish of waters foaming under the wheel. Echoes multiply; myriads of them, faint and far, play peek-a-boo with the solemn pilot, who silently paces the deck when all the ship is wrapped in a deep sleep.

# CHAPTER VII

## Alaskan Village Life

With the morning coffee came a rumor of an Indian village on the neighboring shore. We were already past it, a half hour or more, but canoes were visible. Now this was an episode. Jack, the cabin-boy, slid back the blind; and as I sat up in my bunk, bolstered among the pillows, I saw the green shore, moist with dew and sparkling in the morning light, sweep slowly by – an endless panorama. There is no dust here, not a particle. There is rain at intervals, and a heavy dew-fall, and sometimes a sea fog that makes it highly advisable to suspend all operations until it has lifted. After coffee I found the deck gaily peopled. The steamer was running at half speed; and shortly she took a big turn in a beautiful lagoon and went back on her course far enough to come in sight of the Indian village, but we did not stop there. It seems that one passage we were about to thread was reached at a wrong stage of the tide; and, instead of waiting there for better water, we loafed about for a couple of hours, enjoying it immensely, every soul of us.

Vancouver Island lay upon our left. It was half veiled in mist, or smoke; and its brilliant constellation of sky-piercing peaks, green to the summit, with glints of sunshine gilding the chasms here and there, and rich shadows draping them superbly, reminded me of Nukahiva, one of the Marquesas Islands – the one where Herman Melville found his famed Typee. It seems extravagant to associate any feature in the Alaskan archipelago with the most romantic island in the tropical sea; but there are points of similarity, notwithstanding the geographical discrepancy – daring outlines, magnificent cloud and atmospheric effects, and a fragrance, a pungent balsamic odor ever noticeable. This impalpable, invisible balm permeates everything; it is wafted out over the sea to us, even as the breath of the Spice Islands is borne over the waves to the joy of the passing mariner.

Surely there can be no finer tonic for a fagged fellow with feeble lungs than this glorious Alaskan air. There is no danger of surfeit here; the over-sweet is not likely to be met with in this latitude; and, then, if one really feels the need of change, why, here is a fishing station. The forest is trimmed along the shore so that there is scant room for a few shanties between the water and the wilderness. A dock runs but a little way out into the sea, for the shores are precipitous and one finds a goodly number of fathoms only a few yards from the shingle.

At the top of the dock, sometimes nearly housing the whole of it, stands a shed well stored with barrels, sacks of salt, nets, and all the necessary equipments of a first-class fish-canning establishment. A few Indian lodges are scattered along the shore. The Indians, a hearty and apparently an industrious and willing race, do most of the work about here. A few boats and canoes are drawn up upon the beach. The atmosphere is heavy with the odor of ancient fish. The water-line is strewn with cast-off salmon heads and entrails. Indian dogs and big, fat flies batten there prodigiously. Acres of salmon bellies are rosy in the sun. The blood-red interiors of drying fish – rackfuls of them turned wrong side out – are the only bit of color in all Alaska. Everybody and everything is sombre and subdued.

Yet not all fishing stations are cheerless. The salmon fishery and trading store located at Loring are picturesque. The land-lock nook is as lovely as a Swiss lake; and, oh, the myriad echoes that waken in chorus among these misty mountains! The waters of the Alaskan archipelago are prolific. Vast shoals of salmon, cod, herring, halibut, mullet, ulicon, etc., silver the surface of the sea, and one continually hears the splash of leaping fish.

A traveller has written of his visit to the fishing-grounds on the Naass river, where the tribes had gathered for what is called their "small fishing" – the salmon catch is at another time. These small fish are valuable for food and oil. They run up the river for six weeks only, and with the utmost regularity. At the point he visited, the Naass was about a mile and a half wide; yet so great was the quantity of fish that, with three nails driven into a stick, an Indian would rake up a canoeful in a short time. Five thousand Indians were congregated from British Columbia and Alaska; their faces painted red and black; feathers upon their heads, and imitations of wild beasts upon their dresses. Over the fish was an immense cloud of sea-gulls – so many were there, and so thick were they, that the fluttering of their wings was like a swift fall of snow. Over the gulls were eagles soaring and watching their chance. The halibut, the cod, the porpoise, and the finback whale had followed the little ones out of the deep; and there was confusion worse confounded, and chaos came again in the hours of wild excitement that followed the advent of the small fry, for each and all in sea and air were bent upon the destruction of these little ones.

Seven thousand salmon have been taken at one haul of the seine in this latitude. Most of these salmon weigh sixty pounds each, and some have been caught that weigh a hundred and twenty pounds. Yet there are no game fish in Alaska. Let sportsmen remember that far happier hunting grounds lie within twenty miles of San Francisco, and in almost any district of the Northern or Eastern States. On a certain occasion three of our fellow-voyagers, armed in fashionable fishing toggery, went forth from Sitka for a day's sport. A steam launch bore them to a land where the rank grass and rushes grew shoulder high. Having made their way with difficulty to the margin of a lake, they came upon a boat which required incessant bailing to prevent its speedy foundering. One kept the craft afloat while the others fished until evening. They caught nothing, yet upon landing they found five fish floundering under the seats; these swam in through a hole in the bottom of the boat. I say again, on good authority, there are no game fish in Alaska. There are salmon enough in these waters to supply the world – but the world can be supplied without coming to these waters at all. The truth is, I fear, that the market has been glutted and the business overdone.

One evening we anchored off a sad and silent shore. A few Indian lodges were outlined against the woods beyond. A few Indians stolidly awaited the arrival of a small boat containing one of our fellow-passengers. Then for some hours this boat was busily plying to and fro, bringing out to us all that was portable of a once flourishing, or at least promising, fishery and cannery, now defunct. Meanwhile the mosquitoes boarded our ship on a far more profitable speculation. It was pitiful to see our friend gathering together the *débris* of a wrecked fortune – for he had been wealthy and was now on the down grade of life – hoping almost against hope to be able to turn an honest penny somehow, somewhere, before he dies.

At times we saw solitary canoes containing a whole family of Indians fishing in the watery waste. What solemn lives they must lead! But a more solemn and more solitary scene occurred a little later. All the afternoon we had been sailing under splendid icy peaks. We came in out of the hot sun, and were glad of the cool, snow-chilled air that visited us lightly at intervals.

It was the hour of 9.30 p. m. The sun was dropping behind a lofty mountain range, and in its fine glow we steamed into a lovely cove under a towering height. A deserted, or almost deserted, fishing village stood upon a green bottom land – a mere handful of lodges, with a young growth of trees beyond, and an older growth between these and the glacier that was glistening above them all. A cannery looking nearly new stood at the top of a tall dock on stilts. On the extreme end of the dock was a figure – a man, and a white man at that – with both hands in his pockets, and an attitude of half-awakened curiosity. The figure stood stock-still. We wondered if it lived, if it breathed, or if it was an effigy set up there in scorn of American enterprise. We slowed up and drew near to the dock. It was a curious picture: a half dozen log-built lodges; a few tall piles driven into the land for steamer or trading schooner to make fast to; a group of Indians by a feeble camp fire, – Indians who never once changed their postures more than to wearily lift their heads and regard us with absolute indifference.

When we were near enough to hail the motionless figure on the dock, we did not hail him. Everybody was wildly curious: Everybody was perfectly dumb. The whole earth was silent at last; the wheels had stopped; the boat was scarcely moving through the water. The place, the scene, the hour seemed under a spell. Then a bell rang very shrilly in the deep silence; the paddles plunged into the sea again; we made a graceful sweep under the shadow of the great mountain and proudly steamed away. Not a syllable had been exchanged with that mysterious being on the dock; we merely touched our hats at the last moment; he lifted his, stalked solemnly to the top of the dock and disappeared. There is a bit of Alaskan life for you!

# CHAPTER VIII

## Juneau

Sitka, the capital of Alaska, sleeps, save when she is awakened for a day or two by the arrival of a steamer-load of tourists. Fort Wrangell, the premature offspring of a gold rumor, died, but rose again from the dead when the lust of gold turned the human tide toward the Klondike. Juneau, the metropolis, was the only settlement that showed any signs of vigor before the Klondike day; and she lived a not over-lively village life on the strength of the mines on Douglas Island, across the narrow straits. There were sea-birds skimming the water as we threaded the labyrinthine channels that surround Juneau. We were evidently not very far from the coast-line; for the gulls were only occasional visitors on the Alaskan cruise, though the eagles we had always with us. They soared aloft among the pines that crowned the mountain heights; they glossed their wings in the spray of the sky-tipped waterfalls, and looked down upon us from serene

73

summits with the unwinking eye of scorn. It is awfully fine sailing all about Juneau. Superb heights, snow-capped in many cases, forest-clad in all, and with cloud belts and sunshine mingling in the crystalline atmosphere, form a glorious picture, which, oddly enough, one does not view with amazement and delight, but in the very midst of which, and a very part of which, he is; and the proud consciousness of this marks one of the happiest moments of his life.

Steaming into a lagoon where its mountain walls are so high it seemed like a watery way in some prodigious Venice; steaming in, stealing in like a wraith, we were shortly saluted by the miners on Douglas Island, who are, perhaps, the most persistent and least harmful of the dynamiters. It was not long before we began to get used to the batteries that are touched off every few minutes, night and day; but how strange to find in that wild solitude a 120-stamp mill, electric lights, and all the modern nuisances! Never was there a greater contrast than the one presented at Douglas Island. The lagoon, with its deep, dark waters, still as a dead river, yet mirroring the sea-bird's wing; a strip of beach; just above it rows of cabins and tents that at once suggest the mining camps of early California days; then the rather handsome quarters of the directors; and then the huge mill, admirably constructed and set so snugly among the quarries that it seems almost a part of the ore mountain itself; beyond that the great forest, with its eagles and big game; and the everlasting snow peaks overtopping all, as they lose themselves in the fairest of summer skies. Small boats ply to and fro between Douglas Island and Juneau, a mile or more up the inlet on the opposite shore. These ferries are paddled leisurely, and only the explosive element at Douglas Island gives token of the activity that prevails at Gastineaux Channel.

Soon, weary of the racket on Douglas Island, and expecting to inspect the mine later on, we returned across the water and made fast to the dock in the lower end of Juneau. This settlement has seen a good deal of experience for a young one. It was first known as Pilsbury; then some humorist dubbed it

Fliptown. Later it was called Rockwell and Harrisburg; and finally Juneau, the name it still bears with more or less dignity. The customary Indian village hangs upon the borders of the town; in fact, the two wings of the settlement are aboriginal; but the copper-skin seems not particularly interested in the progress of civilization, further than the occasional chance it affords him of turning an honest penny in the disposal of his wares.

No sooner was the gang-plank out than we all made a rush for the trading stores in search of curios. The faculty of acquisitiveness grows with what it feeds on; and before the Alaskan tour is over, it almost amounts to a mania among the excursionists. You should have seen us – men, women and children – hurrying along the beach toward the heart of Juneau, where we saw flags flying from the staves that stood by the trading-stores. It was no easy task to distance a competitor in those great thoroughfares. Juneau has an annual rainfall of nine feet; the streets are guttered: indeed the streets are gutters in some cases. I know of at least one little bridge that carries the pedestrian from one sidewalk to another, over the muddy road below. I was headed off on my way to the N. W. T. Co.'s warehouse, and sat me down on a stump to write till the rush on bric-a-brac was over. Meanwhile I noticed the shake shanties and the pioneers who hung about them, with their long legs crooked under rush chairs in the diminutive verandas.

Indian belles were out in full feather. Some had their faces covered with a thick coating of soot and oil; the rims of the eyelids, the tip of the nose and the inner portions of the lips showing in striking contrast to the hideous mask, which they are said to wear in order to preserve their complexion. They look for the most part like black-faced monkeys, and appear in this guise a great portion of the time in order to dazzle the town, after a scrubbing, with skins as fair and sleek as soft-soap. Even some of the sterner sex are constrained to resort to art in the hope of heightening their manly beauty; but these are, of course, Alaskan dudes, and as such are doubtless pardonable.

There is a bath-house in Juneau and a barber-shop. They did a big business on our arrival. There are many billiard halls, where prohibited drinks are more or less surreptitiously obtained. A dance-hall stands uninvitingly open to the street. At the doorway, as we passed it, was posted a hand-lettered placard announcing that the ladies of Juneau would on the evening in question give a grand ball in honor of the passengers of the *Ancon*. Tickets, 50 cents.

It began to drizzle. We dodged under the narrow awnings of the shops, and bargained blindly in the most unmusical lingos. Within were to be had stores of toy canoes – graceful little things hewn after the Haida model, with prows and sides painted in strange hieroglyphics; paddles were there – life-size, so to speak, – gorgeously dyed, and just the things for hall decorations; also dishes of carved wood of quaint pattern, and some of them quite ancient, were to be had at very moderate prices; pipes and pipe-bowls of the weirdest description; halibut fish-hooks, looking like anything at all but fish-hooks; Shaman rattles, grotesque in design; Thlinket baskets, beautifully plaited and stained with subdued dyes – the most popular of souvenirs; spoons with bone bowls and handles carved from the horns of the mountain goat or musk-ox; even the big horn-spoon itself was no doubt made by these ingenious people; Indian masks of wood, inlaid with abalone shells, bears' teeth, or lucky stones from the head of the catfish; Indian wampum; deer-skin sacks filled with the smooth, pencil-shaped sticks with which the native sport passes the merry hours away in games of chance; bangles without end, and rings of the clumsiest description hammered out of silver coin; bows and arrows; doll papooses, totem poles in miniature. There were garments made of fish-skins and bird-skins, smelling of oil and semi-transparent, as if saturated with it; and half-musical instruments, or implements, made of twigs strung full of the beaks of birds that clattered with a weird, unearthly Alaskan clatter.

There were little graven images, a few of them looking somewhat idolatrous; and heaps upon heaps of nameless and shapeless odds and ends that boasted more or less bead-work in the line of ornamentation; but all chiefly noticeable for the lack of taste displayed, both in design and the combination of color. The Chilkat blanket is an exception to the Alaskan Indian rule. It is a handsome bit of embroidery, of significant though mysterious design; rich in color, and with a deep, knotted fringe on the lower edge – just the thing for a lambrequin, and to be had in Juneau for $40, which is only $15 more than is asked for the same article in Portland, Oregon, as some of us discovered to our cost. There were quantities of skins miserably cured, impregnating the air with vilest odors; and these were waved at you and wafted after you at every step. In the forest which suddenly terminates at the edge of the town there is game worth hunting. The whistler, reindeer, mountain sheep and goat, ermine, musk-rat, marmet, wolf and bear, are tracked and trapped by the red-man; but I doubt if the foot of the white-man is likely to venture far into the almost impenetrable confusion of logs and brush that is the distinguishing feature of the Alaskan wilderness. Beautiful antlers are to be had in Juneau and elsewhere; and perhaps a cinnamon or a black cub as playful as a puppy, and full of a kind of half-savage fun.

In the upper part of the town, where the stumps and brush are thickest, there are cosy little log-cabins, and garden patches that seem to be making the most of the summer sunshine. In the window of one of these cabins we saw a face – dusky, beautiful, sensitive. Dreamy eyes slumbered under fringes that might have won a song from a Persian poet; admirably proportioned features, delicious lips, almost persuaded us that a squaw-man might in some cases be excusable for his infatuation. Later we discovered that the one beauty of Alaska was of Hawaiian parentage; that she was married, and was as shy of intruders as a caged bird. Very dissimilar are the ladies of Juneau.

In the evening the town-crier went to and fro announcing the opening of the ball. It was still drizzling; the cliffs that tower above the metropolis were capped with cloud; slender, rain-born rivulets plunged from these airy heights into space and were blown away like smoke.

Sometimes we caught glimpses of white, moving objects, far aloft against the black wall of rock: these were mountain sheep.

The cannonading at Douglas Island continued – muffled thunder that ceases neither night nor day. Nobody seemed to think of sleeping. The dock was swarming with Indians; you would have known it with your eyes shut, from the musky odor that permeated every quarter of the ship. The deck was filled with passengers, chatting, reading, smoking, looking off upon the queer little town and wondering what its future was likely to be. And so, we might have lingered on indefinitely, with the light of a dull day above us – a light that was to grow no less till dawn, for there is no night there, – were it not that some one looked at his watch, and lo! it was the midnight hour.

Then we went to the ball given by the ladies of Juneau in our honor. Half a dozen young Indian maidens sat on a bench against the wall and munched peanuts while they smiled; a few straggling settlers gathered at the bar while they smiled; two fiddlers and a guitar made as merry as they could under the circumstances in an alcove at the top of the hall. Round dances were in vogue, – round dances interspersed with flirtations and fire-water; round dances that grew oblong and irregular before sunrise – and yet it was sunrise at the unearthly hour of 3.30 a. m., or thereabout. We all felt as if we had been cheated out of something when we saw his coming; but perhaps it was only the summer siesta that had been cut short, – the summer siesta that here passes for the more wholesome and old-fashioned sleep of the world lower down on the map.

During the night, having discharged freight and exhausted the resources of Juneau, including a post-office, and a post-mistress who sorts the mail twice a month, we steamed back to Douglas Island, and dropped many fathoms of noisy chain into the deep abreast of the camp. The eve of the Fourth in the United States of America is nothing in comparison with the everlasting racket at this wonderful mine. The iron jaws of the 120-stamp mill grind incessantly, spitting pulverized rock and ore into the vats that quake under the mastication of the mighty molars; cars slip down into the bowels of the earth, and emerge laden with precious freight; multitudinous miners relieve one another, watch and watch. Electric light banishes even a thought of dusk; and were it now winter – the long, dark, dreary winter of the North, with but half a dozen hours of legitimate daylight out of the four and twenty – the work at Douglas Island would go on triumphantly; and it will go forever – or, rather, until the bottom drops out of the mine, just as it drops out of everything in this life. All night long the terrible rattle and rumble and roar of the explosive agent robbed us of our rest. I could think of nothing but the gnomes of the German fairy tale; the dwarfs of the black mountain, with their glowworm lamps, darting in and out of the tunnels in the earth like moles, and heaping together the riches that are the cause of so much pleasure and pain, and envy and despair, and sorrow and sin, and too often death.

# CHAPTER IX

# By Solitary Shores

Probably no one leaves Juneau with regret. Far more enjoyable was the day we spent in Ward's Cove, land-locked, wooded to the water's edge, and with forty-five fathoms of water of the richest sea-green hue. Here lay the *Pinta* and the *Paterson*, two characteristic representatives of the United States Navy – as it was before the war – the former a promoted tug-boat, equipped at an expense of $100,000, and now looking top-heavy and unseaworthy, but just the thing for a *matinée* performance of Pinafore, if that were not out of date.

This *Pinta*, terrible as a canal-boat, armed to the teeth, drew up under our quarter to take in coal. You see the *Ancon* combined business with pleasure, and distributed coal in quantities to suit throughout the Alaskan lagoon. Now, there is not much fun in coaling, even when a craft as funny as the *Pinta* is snuggling up under your quarter, looking more like the Pinafore than ever, with her skylarking sailors, midshipmite and all; so Captain Carroll secured a jaunty little steam-launch, and away we went on a picnic in the forest primeval. The launch was laden to the brim; three of our biggest boats were in tow; an abundant collation, in charge of a corps of cabin-boys, gave assurance of success in one line at least.

We explored. Old Vancouver did the same thing long ago, and no doubt found these shores exactly as we find them to-day. We entered a shallow creek at the top of the cove; landed on a dreary point redolent of stale fish, and the beach literally alive and creeping with small worms above half an inch in length. A solitary squaw was splitting salmon for drying. She remained absorbed in her work while we gathered about and regarded her with impudent curiosity. Overcome by the fetid air of the place, we re-embarked and steamed gaily miles away over the sparkling sea.

In an undiscovered country – so it seemed to us – we came to a smooth and sandy strip of shore and landed there. But a few paces from the lightly-breaking ripples was the forest – and such a forest! There were huge trees, looking centuries old, swathed in blankets of moss, and the moss gray with age. Impenetrable depths of shadow overhead, impenetrable depths of litter under foot. Log had fallen upon log crosswise and at every conceivable angle.

Out of the fruitful dust of these deposed monarchs of the forest sprang a numerous progeny – lusty claimants, every one of them, – their foliage feathery and of the most delicate green, being fed only by the thin sunshine that sifts through the dense canopy, supported far aloft by the majestic columns that clustered about us. Under foot the russet moss was of astonishing depth and softness. One walks with care upon it, for the foot breaks through the thick matting that has in many cases spread from log to log, hiding treacherous traps beneath. The ferns luxuriate in this sylvan paradise; and many a beautiful shrub, new to us, bore flowers that blushed unseen until we made our unexpected and perhaps unwelcome appearance.

Here we camped. The cloth was spread in a temple not made with hands; how hard it is to avoid ringing in these little old-time tags about flowers and forests! The viands were deftly served; the merry jest went round, and sometimes came back the same way, "returned with thanks." And thus we revelled in the midst of a solitude that may never before have been broken by the sound of human voice. When we held our peace – which we did at long intervals, and for a brief moment only – we realized this solemn fact; but it didn't seem to impress us much on the spot. Why, even the birds were silent. Only the sea-gulls flashed their white wings under the boughs in the edge of the wood, and wheeled away in dizzy circles, piping sharp, peevish cries.

It was a delightful day we passed together. The memory of it is one of the most precious souvenirs of the Alaskan tour; and it was with reluctance that we returned to the ship, after consulting our watches with astonishment; for the late hours gave no warning, and we might have passed the night there in the loveliest of twilights.

The *Pinta* was about to withdraw to her anchorage as we boarded the *Ancon*; and then, too late, I discovered among the officers of that terror of the sea an old friend with whom I had revelled in the halcyon days at Stag Racket Bungalow, Honolulu. He was then on the U. S. man-of-war, *Alaska* of jolly memory; and he, with his companions, constituted the crack mess of the navy. But the *Alaska* is a sheer hulk, and her once jovial crew scattered hither and yon; he alone, in the solitude of these unfreighted waters, remains to tell the tale. I thought it a happy coincidence that, having met him first under *Old Glory*, then floating in the trade wind that blew over southern seas, I should find him last in the lone land that gave name to the ship that brought him over. Can the theosophists unravel this mystery, or see aught in it that verges upon the mystic philosophy? As we steamed out of Wood's Cove that night, with the echoes of a parting salute filling the heavens to overflowing, we saw a cluster of small, dark islets in the foreground; shining waters beyond flowed to the foot of far-away mountains; a silvery sky melted into gold as it neared the horizon: this picture, as delicate in tint as the most exquisite water-color, was framed in a setting of gigantic pines; and it was by this fairy portal we entered the sea of ice.

From solitude to solitude is the order in Alaska. The solitude of the forest and the sea, of the mountain and ravine, – with these we had become more or less familiar when our good ship headed for the solitude of ice and snow. I began to feel as if we were being dragged out on the roof of the world – as if we were swimming in the flooded eaves of a continent. Sometimes there came over me a sense of loneliness – of the distance that lay between us and everybody else, and of the helplessness of our case should any serious accident befall us. It is this very state, perhaps, that ages the hearts of the hardiest of the explorers who seek vainly to unravel the polar mystery.

From time to time as we sailed, the sea, now a brighter blue than ever, was strewn with fragments of ice. Very lovely they looked as they hugged the distant shore; a ghostly and fantastical procession, borne ever southward by the slow current; and growing more ghostly and fantastical hour by hour, as they dwindled in the clear sunshine of the long summer days. Anon the ice fragments increased in number and dimensions. The whole watery expanse was covered with brash, and we were obliged to pick our way with considerable caution. At times we narrowly escaped grazing small icebergs, that might have disabled us had we come in collision with them. As it was, many an ice-cake that looked harmless enough, being very low in the water, struck us with a thud that was startling; or passed under our old-fashioned side-wheels, splintering the paddles and causing our hearts to leap within us. A disabled wheel meant a tedious delay in a latitude where the resources are decidedly limited. Often we thought of the miserable millions away down East simmering in the sultry summer heat, while the thermometer with us stood at 45 degrees in the sun, and the bracing salt air was impregnated with balsamic odors.

In this delectable state we sighted a bouncing baby iceberg, and at once made for it with the enthusiasm of veritable discoverers. It was pretty to see with what discretion we approached and circled round it, searching for the most favorable point of attack. So much of an iceberg is beneath the surface of the water, ballasting the whole, that it is rather ticklish business cruising in its vicinity. We lay off and on, coquetting with the little beauty, while one of our boats pulled up to it, and threw a lariat over a glittering peak that flamed in the sun like a torch. Then we drew in the slack and made fast, while a half dozen of our men mounted the slippery mass, armed with ropes and axes, and began to hack off big chunks, which were in due season transferred to our iceboxes.

Our iceberg was about fifty feet in length and twenty or thirty feet out of the water. It was a glittering island, with savage peaks, deep valleys, bluffs, and promontories. The edges were delicately frilled and resembled silver filigree. Some of these, which were transparent and as daintily turned as old Venetian glass, dripped continually like rain-beaten eaves. The portion nearest the water's edge was honeycombed by the wavelets that dashed upon it without ceasing, rushing in and out of the small, luminous caverns in swift, sparkling rivulets. Much of the surface was crusted with a fine frosting; it was full of wells deep enough to sink a man in. These wells were filled with water, and with a blue light, celestial in its loveliness, – a light ethereal and pellucid. It was as if the whole iceberg were saturated with transfused moonbeams, that gave forth a mellow radiance, which flashed at times like brilliants, and burst into flame and played like lightning along the almost invisible rims and ridges. The unspeakable, the incomprehensible light throbbed through and through; and was sometimes bluish green and sometimes greenish blue; but oftenest with the one was the other, both at once, and with a perfectly bewildering tint added, – in a word, it was frozen moonlight and no mistake. O my friend, I assure you there are many famous sports with not half the fun in them that there is in lassoing an iceberg!

Once more I turn to my note-books. I find that the morning had been foggy; that we could see scarcely a ship's length ahead of us; that the water was like oil beneath and the mists like snow above and about, while we groped blindly. Of course we could not press forward under the circumstances; for we were surrounded by islands great and small, and any one of these might silently materialize at a moment's notice; but we were not idle. Now and again our paddles beat the water impetuously, and they hung dripping, while the sea stretched around us as we leisurely drifted on like a larger bubble in danger of bursting upon an unexpected rock. We sounded frequently. There was an abundance of water – there nearly always is throughout the Alaskan archipelago; enough and to spare; but the abrupt shore might be but a stone's-throw from us on the one hand or the other.

What was to be done? In the vast stillness we blew a blast on our shrill whistle, and listened for the echo. Sometimes it returned to us almost on the instant and we cried, "Halt!" When we halted or veered off, creeping as it were on the surface of the oily sea, sometimes a faint or far-off whisper – "the horns of elf-land" – gave us assurance of plenty of space and the sea-room we were sorely in need of just then. Once we saw looming right under our prow a little islet with a tuft of fir-trees crowning it – the whole worthy to be made the head-piece or tail-piece to some poem on solitude. It was very picturesque; but it seemed to be crouching there, lying in wait for us, ready to arch its back the moment we came within reach. The rapidity with which we backed out of that predicament left us no time for apologies.

Again we got some distance up the wrong channel. When the fog lifted for a moment, we discovered the error, put about without more ado, and went around the block in a hurry. Meanwhile we had schooled our ears to detect the most delicate shades of sound; to measure or weigh each individual echo with an accuracy that gave us the utmost self-satisfaction. Perhaps Captain Carroll or Captain George, who was spying out the land with his ears, would not have trusted the ship in our keeping for five minutes – but no matter.

Presently the opaque atmosphere began to dissolve away; and as the sun brushed the webs from his face, and darted sharp beams upon the water all at once in a shower, the fog-banks went to pieces and rolled away in sections out of sight, like the transformation scene in a Christmas pantomime. And there we were in the very centre of the smiling island world, with splendid snow peaks towering all about us; and such a flood of blue sky and bluer water, golden sunshine and gilded fields of snow, of jutting shores clad in perennial verdure, and eagles and sea-birds wheeling round about us, as can be seen nowhere else in the wide world to the same advantage.

We were entering a region of desolation. The ice was increasing, and the water took that ghastly hue, even a glimpse of which is enough to chill the marrow in one's bones. Vegetation was dying out. A canoe-full of shivering Indians were stemming the icy flood in search of some chosen fishery, – all of them blanketed, and all – squaw as well as papooses – taking a turn at the paddle. These were the children of Nature, whose song-birds are the screaming eagle, the croaking raven, and the crying sea-doves blown inland by the wild westerly gales.

We were now nearly within sound of the booming glaciers; and as we drew nearer and nearer I could but brood over the oft imagined picture of that vast territory – our Alaska, – where, beyond that mountain range, the almost interminable winter is scarcely habitable, and the summers so brief it takes about six of them to make a swallow.

# CHAPTER X

## In Search of the Totem-Pole

Hour after hour and day after day we are coasting along shores that become monotonous in their beauty. For leagues the sea-washed roots of the forest present a fairly impassable barrier to the foot of man. It is only at infrequent intervals that a human habitation is visible, and still more seldom does the eye discover a solitary canoe making its way among the inextricable confusion of inlets. Sometimes a small cluster of Indian lodges enlivens the scene; and this can scarcely be said to enliven it, for most Indian lodges are as forlorn as a last year's bird's-nest. Sometimes a bright little village gives hope of a break in the serenity of the season – a few hours on shore and an extra page or two in our log-books. Yet again, sometimes it is a green jungle, above the sea, out of which rise diminutive box-houses, like exaggerated dove-cotes, with a goodly number of towering cedar columns, curiously carved, perhaps stained black or red in patches, scattered through them. These are Indian cemeteries. They are hedged about with staves, from the top of which flutter ragged streamers. They are rich in rude carvings of men and birds and beasts. Now and again a shield as big as a target, and looking not unlike an archery-target, marks the tomb of some warrior. The unerring shafts of death search out the obscurest handfuls of people scattered through these wide domains; and every village has its solemn suburb, where the houses of the dead are decorated with barbaric bric-a-brac.

Many of the tombs are above ground – airy sarcophagi on high poles rocking in the wind and the rain. Some are nearer the earth, like old-fashioned four-poster bed-steads; and there the dead sleep well. Others are of stone, with windows and peaked roofs, – very comfortable receptacles. But most of the bodies are below ground, and the last vestiges of their graves are lost in the depths of the jungle. Incineration is not uncommon in Alaska, and in such cases the ashes are distributed among the winds and waves. Birds feast upon the bodies of certain tribes – meat-offerings, very gracious in the sight of the Death Angel; but by far the larger portion find decent burial, and they are all long and loudly and sincerely mourned.

We awoke one morning at Casa-an, and found ourselves made fast to a dock. On the dock was a salmon-house, or shed, a very laboratory of ancient and fish-like smells. It was not long before the tide slipped away from us and left the steamer resting easily on her beam-ends in shallow water. We were prisoners for a few hours; but we were glad of this, for every hour was of interest to us. This was our first chance to thoroughly explore an Indian village; and, oh! the dogs, cousins-german to the coyotes, that shook off their fleas and bayed us dismally! Lodges of the rudest sort were scattered about in the most convenient localities. As for streets or lanes, there were none visible. The majority of the lodges were constructed of hemlock bark or of rough slabs, gaudily festooned with split salmon drying in the sun. The lodges are square, with roofs slightly inclined; they are windowless and have but one narrow door about shoulder high.

The Casa-an Indians are a tribe of the Haidas, the cleverest of the northern races. They are expert craftsmen. From a half dollar they will hammer out or mold a bangle and cover it with chasing very deftly cut. Their wood-carvings, medicine-man rattles, spoons, broth bowls, and the like, are curious; but the demand for bangles keeps the more ingenious busy in this branch of industry. Unfortunately, some simple voyager gave the rude silversmiths a bangle of the conventional type, and this is now so cunningly imitated that it is almost impossible to secure a specimen of Haida work of the true Indian pattern. Very shortly the Indian villages of Alaska will be stocked with curios of genuine California manufacture. The supply of antiquities and originals has been already nearly, if not quite, exhausted. It is said that no sooner is the boom of the paddle-wheel heard in the noiseless Alaskan sea than the Indian proceeds to empty of its treasures his cedar chest or his red Chinese box studded with brass nails, and long before the steamer heaves in sight the primitive bazar is ready for the expected customer. There is much haggling over the price of a curio, and but little chance of a bargain. If one has his eye upon some coveted object, he had best purchase it at once at the first figure; for the Indian is not likely to drop a farthing, and there are others who will gladly outbid the hesitating shopper.

Time is no object in the eyes of these people. If an Indian thought he could make a quarter more on the sale of a curio by holding it a month longer, until the arrival of the next excursion boat, or even by getting into his canoe and paddling a day or two over to the next settlement, he would as lief do it as not. By the merest chance I drew from a heap of rubbish in the corner of a lodge a Shaman rattle, unquestionably genuine. This Shaman rattle is a quaintly carved rattle-box, such as is used by sorcerers or medicine-men in propitiation of the evil spirit at the bedside of the dying. The one I have was not offered for sale, nor did the possessor seem to place much value on it; yet he would not budge one jot or tittle in the price he first set upon it, and seemingly set at a guess. Its discovery was a piece of pure luck, but I would not exchange it for any other curio which I chanced to see during the whole voyage.

In one of the lodges at Casa-an a chief lay dying. He was said to be the last of his race; and, judging from appearances, his hours were fast drawing to a close. He was breathing painfully; his face was turned to the wall. Two or three other Indians sat silently about, stirring at intervals a bright wood-fire that burned in the centre of the lodge. The curling smoke floated gracefully through a hole in the roof – most of it, but not quite all. As we entered (we were in search of the dying chief; for, as he seemed to be the one lion in the settlement, his fame was soon noised abroad) we found that the evangelist had forestalled us. He was asking the price of salmon in San Francisco; but upon our appearance he added, solemnly enough: "Well, we all must die – Indians and all." An interpreter had reluctantly been pressed into service; but as the missionary work was not progressing, the evangelist dropped the interpreter, rolled up his spiritual sleeves and pitched in as follows:

"Say, you Injun! you love God? You love Great Spirit?" No answer came from the thin, drawn lips, tightly compressed and visible just over the blankets edge in the corner of the lodge. "Say, John! you ready to die! You make your peace with God! You go to heaven – to the happy hunting-ground?" The chief, who had silenced the interpreter with a single look, was apparently beyond the hearing of human speech; so the evangelist, with a sigh, again inquired into the state of the salmon market on the Pacific coast. Then the stricken brave turned a glazed eye upon the man of God, and the latter once more sought to touch that heart of stone: "I say, you Injun! you prepared to meet Great Spirit? You ready to go to happy hunting-ground?" The chief's eyes flamed for a moment, as with infinite scorn he muttered between his teeth to the evangelist: "You ---- fool! You go to ----!" And he went.

While the steamer was slowly righting we had ample time to inspect the beached hull of a schooner with a history. She was the Pioneer of Casa-an once commanded by a famous old smuggler named Baronovich. Long he sailed these waters; and, like Captain Kidd, he bore a charmed life as he sailed. It is a mystery to me how any sea-faring man can trust his craft to the mercy of the winds and tides of this myriad-islanded inland sea. This ancient mariner, Baronovich, not only braved the elements, but defied Russian officials, who kept an eye upon him night and day. On one occasion, having been boarded by the vigilant inspectors, and his piratical schooner thoroughly searched from stem to stern, he kindly invited the gentlemen to dine with him, and entertained them at a board groaning with the contraband luxuries which his suspicious guests had been vainly seeking all the afternoon. It is a wee little cabin and a shallow hold that furnish the setting for a sea-tale as wildly picturesque as any that thrills the heart of your youthful reader; but high and dry lies the moldering hulk of the dismantled smuggler, and there is no one left to tell the tale.

As we lounged about, some hideous Indians – I trust they were not framed in the image of their Maker, – ill-shapen lads, dumpy, expressionless babies, green-complexioned half-breeds, sat and looked on with utter indifference. Many of the Haida Indians have kinky or wavy hair, Japanese or Chinese eyes, and most of them toe out; but they are, all things considered, the least interesting, the most ungainly and the most unpicturesque of people. If there is work for them to do they do it, heedless of the presence of inquisitive, pale-faced spectators. Indeed they seem to look down upon the white-man, and perhaps they have good reasons for so doing. If there is no work to be done, they are not at all disconcerted.

I very much doubt if a Haida Indian – or any other Indian, for that matter – knows what it is to be bored or to find the time hanging heavily on his hands. I took note of one old Indian who sat for four solid hours without once changing his position. He might have been sitting there still but that his wife routed him out after a lively monologue, to which he was an apparently disinterested listener. At last he arose with a grunt, adjusted his blanket, strode grimly to his canoe and bailed it out; then he entered and paddled leisurely to the opposite shore, where he disappeared in the forest.

Filth was everywhere, and evil odors; but far, far aloft the eagles were soaring, and the branches of a withered tree near the settlement were filled with crows as big as buzzards. Once in awhile some one or another took a shot at them – and missed. Thus the time passed at Casa-an. One magnifies the merest episode on the Alaskan voyage, and is grateful for it.

Killisnoo is situated in a cosy little cove. It is a rambling village that climbs over the rocks and narrowly escapes being pretty, but it manages to escape. Most of the lodges are built of logs, have small, square windows, with glass in them, and curtains; and have also a kind of primitive chimney. We climbed among these lodges and found them quite deserted. The lodgers were all down at the dock. There were inscriptions on a few of the doors: the name of the tenant, and a request to observe the sacredness of the domestic hearth. This we were careful to do; but inasmuch as each house was set in order and the window-curtains looped back, we were no doubt welcome to a glimpse of an Alaskan interior. It was the least little bit like a peep-show, and didn't seem quite real. One inscription was as follows – it was over the door of the lodge of the laureate:

JOSEPH HOOLQUIN.

My tum-tum is white,
I try to do right:
All are welcome to come
To my hearth and my home.
So call in and see me, white, red or black man:
I'm de-late hyas of the Kootznahoo quan.

Need I add that *tum-tum* in the Chinook jargon signifies the soul! Joseph merely announced that he was clean-souled; also *de-late hyas* – that is, above reproach.

At the store of the Northwest Trading Company we found no curios, and it is the only store in the place. Sarsaparilla, tobacco, blankets, patent medicines, etc., are there neatly displayed on freshly painted shelves, but no curios. On a strip of plank walk in front of the place are Indians luxuriously heaped, like prize porkers, and they are about as interesting a spectacle to the unaccustomed eye.

Our whistle blew at noon. We returned on board, taking the cannery and oil-factory on the way, and finding it impossible to forget them for some time afterward. At 12.45 p. m. we were off, but we left one of the merriest and most popular of our voyagers behind us. He remained at Killisnoo in charge of the place. As we swam off into the sweet sea reaches, the poor fellow ran over the ridge of his little island, looking quite like a castaway, and no doubt feeling like one. He sprang from rock to rock and at last mounted a hillock, and stood waving his arms wildly while we were in sight. And the lassies? They swarmed like bees upon the wheelhouse, wringing their hands and their handkerchiefs, and weeping rivers of imaginary tears over our first bereavement! But really, now, what a life to lead, and in what a place, especially if one happens to be young, and good-looking and a bit of a swell withal!

But is there no romance here? Listen! We came to anchor over night in a quiet nook where the cliffs and the clouds overshadowed us. Everything was of the vaguest description, without form and void. There seemed to be one hut on shore, with the spark of a light in it – a cannery of course. Canoes were drifting to and fro like motes in the darkness, tipped with a phosphorescent rim. Indian voices hailed us out of the ominous silence; Indian dogs muttered under their breath, yelping in a whisper which was mocked by Indian papooses, who can bark before they have learned to walk or talk.

Softly out of the balmy night – for it was balmy and balsamic (we were to the windward of the cannery), – a shadowy canoe floated up just under our rail; two shadowy forms materialized, and voices like the voices of spirits – almost the softest voices in the world, voices of infantile sweetness – hailed us. "*Alah, mika chahko!*" babbled the flowers of the forest. My solitary companion responded glibly, for he was no stranger in these parts. The maids grew garrulous. There was much bantering, and such laughter as the gods delight in; and at last a shout that drew the attention of the captain. He joined us just in season to recognize the occupants of the canoe, as they shot through a stream of light under an open port, crying "*Anah nawitka mika halo shem!*" And then we learned that the sea-nymphs he had put to flight were none other than the belles of Juneau City, the Alaskan metropolis, who were spending the summer at this watering-place, and who were known to fame as "Kitty the Gopher," and "Feather-Legged Sal."

# CHAPTER XI

## In the Sea of Ice

We appreciated the sun's warmth so long as we were cruising among the ice-wrack. Some of the passengers, having been forewarned, were provided with heavy overcoats, oilskin hats, waterproofs, woolen socks, and stogies with great nails driven into the soles. They were iron-bound, copper-fastened tourists, thoroughly equipped – Alpine-stock and all, – and equal to any emergency.

Certainly it rains whenever it feels like it in Alaska. It can rain heavily for days together, and does so from time to time. The excursion-boat may run out of one predicament into another, and the whole voyage be a series of dismal disappointments; but this is not to be feared. The chances are in favor of a round of sunshiny days and cloudless nights as bright as the winter days in New England; of the fairest of fair weather; bracing breezes tempered by the fragrant forests that mantle each of the ten thousand islands; cool nights in midsummer, when a blanket is welcome in one's bunk; a touch of a fog now and again, generally lasting but a few hours, and welcome, also, by way of change. As for myself, a rubber coat protected me in the few showers to which we were exposed, and afforded warmth enough in the coldest weather we encountered. For a climb over a glacier, the very thickest shoes are absolutely necessary; beyond these, all else seems superfluous to me, and the superfluous is the chief burden of travel.

We were gathered about the deck in little groups. The unpremeditated coteries which naturally spring into existence on shipboard hailed one another across decks, from the captain's cabin – a favorite resort – or the smoking-room, as we sighted objects of interest. With us there was no antagonism, albeit we numbered a full hundred, and for three weeks were confined to pretty close quarters. Passing the hours thus, and felicitating ourselves upon the complete success of the voyage, we were in the happiest humor, and amiably awaited our next experience.

Presently we ran under a wooded height that shut off the base of a great snow-capped mountain. The peak was celestial in its beauty, – a wraith dimly outlined upon the diaphanous sky, of which it seemed a more palpable part. When we had rounded this point we came face to face with a glacier. We saw at a glance the length and the breadth of it as it plowed slowly down between lofty rock-ridges to within a mile and a half of the shore. This was our first sight of one of those omnipotent architects of nature, and we watched it with a thrill of awe.

Picture to yourself a vast river, two or three miles in breadth, pouring down from the eminence of an icy peak thirty miles away, – a river fed by numerous lateral tributaries that flow in from every declivity. Imagine this river lashed to a fury and covered from end to end, fathoms deep, with foam, and then the whole suddenly frozen and fixed for evermore – that is your glacier. Sometimes the surface is stained with the *débris* of the mountain; sometimes the bluish-green tinge of the ancient ice crops out. Generally the surface is as white as down and very fair to look upon; for at a distance – we were about eight miles from the lower edge of it – the eye detects no flaw. It might be a torrent of milk and honey. It might almost be compared in its immaculate beauty to one of the rivers of Paradise that flow hard by the throne of God. It seems to be moving in majesty, and yet is stationary, or nearly so; for we might sit by its frozen shore and grow gray with watching, and ever our dull eyes could detect no change in a ripple of it. A river of Paradise, indeed, escaped from the gardens of the blessed; but, overcome by the squalor of this little globe, it has stopped short and turned to ice in its alabaster bed.

One evening, about 8.30 o'clock, the sun still high above the western mountain range, we found ourselves opposite the Davidson glacier. It passes out of a broad ravine and spreads fanlike upon the shore under the neighboring cliffs. It is three miles in breadth along the front, and is twelve hundred feet in height when it begins to crumble and slope toward the shore. A terminal moraine, a mile and a half in depth, separates it from the sea. A forest, or the remnant of a forest, stands between it and the water it is slowly but surely approaching. The fate of this solemn wood is sealed. Anon the mightiest among these mighty trees will fall like grain before the sickle of the reaper.

We are very near this glacier. We see all the wrinkles and fissures and the deep discolorations. We see how the monstrous mass winds in and out between the mountains, and crowds them on every side, and rubs their skin off in spots, and leaves grooved lines, like high-water marks, along the face of the cliffs; how it gathers as it goes, and grinds to powder and to paste whatever comes within its reach, growing worse and worse, and greedier and more rapacious as it creeps down into the lowlands; so that when it reaches the sea, where it must end its course and dissolve away, it will have covered itself with slime and confusion. It will have left ruin and desolation in its track, but it will likewise have cleft out a valley with walls polished like brass and a floor as smooth as marble, – one that will be utilized in after ages, when it has carpeted itself with green and tapestried its walls with vines. Surely no other power on earth could have done the job so neatly.

One sees this work in process and in fresh completion in Alaska. The bald islet yonder, with a surface as smooth as glass and with delicate tracery along its polished sides – tracery that looks like etching upon glass, – was modelled by glaciers not so many years ago: within the century, some of them, perhaps. A glacier – probably the very glacier we are seeking – follows this track and grinds them all into shape. Every angle of action – of motion, shall I say? – is indelibly impressed upon each and every rock here about; so all these northlands, from sea to sea, the world over, have been laboriously licked into shape by the irresistible tide of ice. Verily, the mills of the gods grind slowly, but what a grist they grind!

Let me record an episode that occasioned no little excitement among the passengers and crew of the *Ancon*. While we were picking our way among the floating ice – and at a pretty good jog, too, – a dark body was seen to fall from an open port, forward, into the sea. There was a splash and a shriek as it passed directly under the wheel and disappeared in the foam astern. "Man overboard!" was the cry that rang through the ship, while we all rushed breathlessly to the after-rail. Among the seething waters in our wake, we saw a head appearing and disappearing, and growing smaller and smaller all the while, though the swimmer was struggling bravely to hold his own. In a moment the engines were stopped; and then – an after-thought – we made as sharp a turn as possible, hoping to lessen the distance between us, while a boat was being manned and lowered for the rescue. We feared that it was the cook, who was running a fair chance of being drowned or chilled to death. His black head bobbed like a burnt cork on the crest of the waves; and, though we marked a snow-white circle in the sea, we seemed to get no nearer the strong swimmer in his agony; and all at once we saw him turn, as in desperation or despair, and make for one of the little rocky islets that were lying at no great distance. Evidently he believed himself deserted, and was about to seek this desolate rock in the hope of prolonging existence.

By this time we had come to a dead halt, and a prolonged silence followed. Our sailor boys pulled lustily at the oars; yet the little boat seemed to crawl through yawning waves, and, as usual, every moment was an hour of terrible suspense. Then the captain, the most anxious among us all, made a trumpet of his hands and shouted: "Here, Pete, old boy! Here, Pete, you black rascal!" At the sound of his voice the swimmer suddenly turned and struck out for the ship with an enthusiasm that was actually ludicrous. We roared with laughter – we could not help it; for when the boat had pulled up to the almost water-logged swimmer, and he began to climb in with an energy that imperiled the safety of the crew, we saw that the black rascal in question was none other than Pete Bruin, Captain Carroll's pet bear. He shook himself and drenched the oarsmen, who were trying to get him back to the ship; for he was half frantic with delight, and it was pretty close quarters – a small boat in a chop sea dotted with lumpy ice; and a frantic bear puffing and blowing as he shambled bear-fashion from the stem to stern, and raised his voice at intervals in a kind of hoarse "hooray," that depressed rather than cheered his companions. It was ticklish business getting the boat and its lively crew back to the davits in safety.

It was still more ticklish receiving the shaggy hero on deck; for he gave one wild bound and alighted in the midst of a group of terrified ladies and scattered the rest of us in dismay. But it was side-splitting when the little fellow, seeing an open door, made a sudden break for it, and plunged into the berth of a shy damsel, who, put to ignominious flight in the first gust of the panic, had sought safety in her state-room only to be singled out for the recipient of the rascal's special attentions. She was rescued by the bravest of the brave; but Bruin had to be dragged from behind the lace curtains with a lasso, and then he brought some shreds of lace with him as a trophy. He was more popular than ever after this little adventure, and many an hour we spent in recounting to one another the varied emotions awakened by the episode.

Heading for Glacier Bay, we found a flood of bitter cold water so filled with floating ice that it was quite impossible to avoid frequent collisions with masses of more or less magnitude. There was an almost continual thumping along the ship's side as the paddle struck heavily the ice fragments which we found littering the frozen sea. There was also a dull reverberation as of distant thunder that rolled over the sea to us; and when we learned that this was the crackling of the ice-pack in the gorges, we thought with increasing solemnity of the majesty of the spectacle we were about to witness.

Thus we pushed forward bravely toward an ice-wall that stretched across the top of the bay from one high shore to the other. This wall of ice, a precipitous bluff or palisade, is computed to be from two hundred to five hundred feet in height. It is certainly nowhere less than two hundred, but most of it far nearer five hundred feet above sea level, rising directly out of it, overhanging it, and chilling the air perceptibly. Picking our path to within a safe distance of the glacier, we cast anchor and were free to go our ways for a whole glorious day. According to Professor John Muir – for whom the glacier is deservedly named, – the ice-wall measures three miles across the front; ten miles farther back it is ten miles in breadth. Sixteen tributary glaciers unite to form the one.

Professor Muir, accompanied by the Rev. S. Hall Young, of Fort Wrangell, visited it in 1879. They were the first white men to explore this region, and they went thither by canoe. Muir, with blankets strapped to his back and his pockets stuffed with hard-tack, spent days in rapturous speculation. Of all glacial theorists he is doubtless the most self-sacrificing and enthusiastic. I believe, as yet, no one has timed this glacier. It is dissolving away more rapidly than it travels; so that although it is always advancing, it seems in reality to be retreating.

Within the memory of the last three

generations the Muir glacier filled the bay for miles below our anchorage; and while it recedes, it is creeping slowly down, scalping the mountains, grinding all the sharp edges into powder or leaving a polished surface behind it. It gathers rock dust and the wreck of every living thing, and mixes them up with snow and ice. These congeal again, or are compressed into soft, filthy monumental masses, waiting their turn to topple into the waves at last. The wash of the sea undermines the glacier; the sharp sunbeams blast it. It is forever sinking, settling, crushing in upon itself and splitting from end to end, with fearful and prolonged intestinal reverberations, that remind one of battle thunders and murder and sudden death. There was hardly a moment during the day free from rumble or a crash or a splash.

The front elevation might almost be compared to Niagara Falls in winter; but here is a spectacular effect not often visible at Niagara. At intervals huge fragments of the ice cliffs fall, carrying with them torrents of snow and slush. Heaven only knows know many hundred thousand tons of this *débris* plunged into the sea under our very eyes. Nor was it all *débris*: there were masses of solid ice so lustrous they looked like gigantic emeralds or sapphires, and these were fifty or even a hundred times the size of our ship. When they fell they seemed to descend with the utmost deliberation; for they fell a much greater distance than we could realize, as their bulk was beyond conception, so that a fall of two hundred or three hundred feet seemed not a tenth part of that distance.

With this deliberate descent, as if they floated down, they also gave an impression of vast weight and when they struck the sea, the foam flew two-thirds of the way up the cliff – a fountain three hundred feet in height and of monstrous volume. Then after a long time – a very long time it seemed to us – the ice would rise slowly from the deep and climb the face of the cliff as if it were about to take its old place again; but it sank and rose, until it had found its level, when it joined the long procession drifting southward to warmer waves and dissolution.

In the meantime the ground swell that followed each submersion resembled a tidal wave as it rolled down upon us and threatened to engulf us. But the *Ancon* rode like a duck – I can not consistently say swan in this case, – and heaved to starboard and to larboard in picturesque and thoroughly nautical fashion. Some of us were on shore, wading in the mud and the slush, or climbing the steep bluffs that hem in the glacier upon one side. Here it was convenient to glance over the wide, wide snow-fields that seem to have been broken with colossal harrows. It was even possible to venture out upon the ice ridges, leaping the gaps that divided them in every direction. But at any moment the crust might have broken and buried us from sight; and we found the spectacle far more enjoyable when viewed from the deck of the steamer.

What is that glacier like? Well, just a little like the whitewashed crater of an active volcano. At any rate, it is the glorious companion piece to Kilauea in Hawaii. In these wonders of nature you behold the extremes, fire and ice, having it all their own way, and a world of adamant shall not prevail against them.

# CHAPTER XII

## Alaska's Capital

Sitka has always seemed to me the jumping-off place. I have vaguely imagined that somehow – I know not just how – it had a mysterious affinity with Moscow, and was in some way a dependence of that Muscovite municipality. I was half willing to believe that an underground passage connected the Kremlin with the Castle of Sitka; that the tiny capital of Great Alaska responded, though feebly, to every throb of the Russian heart. Perhaps it did in the good old days now gone; but there is little or nothing of the Russian element left, and the place is as dead as dead can be without giving offence to the olfactory organ.

We were picking our way through a perfect wilderness of islands, on the lookout for the capital, of which we had read and heard so much. Surely the Alaskan pilot must have the eye and the instinct of a sea bird or he could never find a port in that labyrinth. Moreover, the air was misty: we felt that we were approaching the sea. Lofty mountains towered above us; sometimes the islands swam apart – they seemed all in motion, as if they were swinging to and fro on the tide, – and then down a magnificent vista we saw the richly wooded slopes of some glorious height that loomed out of the vapor and bathed its forehead in the sunshine. Sometimes the mist grew denser, and we could see hardly a ship's-length ahead of us; and the air was so chilly that our overcoats were drawn snugly about us, and we wondered what the temperature might be "down south" in Dakota and New England.

In the grayest of gray days we came to Sitka, and very likely for this reason found it a disappointment at first sight. Certainly it looked dreary enough as we approached it – a little cluster of tumbledown houses scattered along a bleak and rocky shore. We steamed slowly past it, made a big turn in deep water, got a tolerable view of the city from one end of it to the other, and then crept up to the one little dock, made fast, and were all granted the freedom of the capital for a couple of days. It is a gray place – gray with a greenish tinge in it – the kind of green that looks perennial – a dark, dull evergreen.

There was some show of color among the costumes of the people on shore – bright blankets and brighter calicoes, – but there was no suspicion of gaiety or of a possible show of enthusiasm among the few sedate individuals who came down to see us disembark. I began to wonder if these solemn spectators that were grouped along the dock were ghosts materialized for the occasion; if the place were literally dead – dead as the ancient Russian cemetery on the hill, where the white crosses with their double arms, the upper and shorter one aslant, shone through the sad light of the waning day.

We had three little Russian maids on our passenger list, daughters of Father Mitropolski, the Greek priest at Sitka. They were returning from a convent school at Victoria, and were bubbling over with delight at the prospective joys of a summer vacation at home. But no sooner had they received the paternal embraces upon the deck than the virtue of happiness went out of them; and they became sedate little Sitkans, whose dignity belied the riotous spirit that had made them the life of the ship on the way up.

We also brought home a little Russian chap who had been working down at Fort Wrangell, and, having made a fortune – it was a fortune in his eyes, – he was returning to stay in the land of his nativity. He was quiet enough on shipboard – indeed, he had almost escaped observation until we sighted Sitka; but then his heart could contain itself no longer, and he made confidants of several of us to whom he had spoken never a word until this moment. How glad he was to greet its solemn shores, to him the dearest spot in all the earth! A few hours later we met him. He was swinging on the gate at the homestead in the edge of the town: a sweet, primitive place, that caught our eye before the youngster caught our ears with his cheerful greeting. "Oh, I so glad!" said he, with a mist in his eye that harmonized with everything else. "I make eighty dollar in four month at

Wrangell. My sister not know me when I get home. I so glad to come back to Sitka. I not go away any more."

Of course we poured out of the ship in short order, and spread through the town like ants. At the top of the dock is the Northwest Trading Company's store – how we learned to know these establishments! Some scoured it for a first choice, and got the pick of the wares; but here, as elsewhere, we found the same motley collection of semi-barbarous bric-a-brac – brilliantly painted Indian paddles spread like a sunburst against the farther wall; heaps of wooden masks and all the fantastical carvings such as the aborigines delight in, and in which they almost excel. Up the main street of the town is another store, where a series of large rooms, crowded with curios bewilders the purchaser of those grotesque wares.

At the top of Katalan's rock, on the edge of the sea, stands the Colonial Castle. It is a wooden structure, looking more like a barrack than a castle. At the foot of the rock are the barracks and Custom House. A thin sprinkling of marines, a few foreign-looking citizens – the full-fledged Rusk of the unmistakable type is hard to find nowadays, – and troops of Indians give a semblance of life to this quarter. At the head of the street stands the Russian Orthodox Church; and this edifice, with its quaint tower and spire, is really the lion of the place. St. Michael's was dedicated in 1844 by the Venerable Ivan Venianimoff, the metropolitan of Moscow, for years priest and Bishop at Ounalaska and Sitka.

In his time the little chapel was richly decorated; but as the settlement began falling to decay, the splendid vestments and sacred vessels and altar ornaments, and even the Bishop himself, were transferred to San Francisco. It then became the duty of the Bishop to visit annually the churches at Sitka, Ounalaska and Kodiak, as the Russian Government still allowed these dependencies an annuity of $50,000. But the last incumbent of the office, Bishop Nestor, was lost tragically at sea in May, 1883; and, as the Russian priesthood seems to be less pious than particular, the office is still a-begging – unless I have been misinformed.

Probably the mission will be abandoned. Certainly the dilapidated chapel, with its remnants of tarnished finery, its three surviving families of Russian blood, its handful of Indian converts, seems not likely to hold long together.

We witnessed a service in St. Michael's. The tinkling bells in the green belfry – a bulbous, antique-looking belfry it is – rang us in from the four quarters of the town. As there were neither pews, chairs nor prayer carpets, we stood in serio-comic silence while the double mysteries of the hidden Holy of Holies were celebrated. Not more than a dozen devotees at most were present. These gathered modestly in the rear of the nave and put us to shame with their reverent gravity. Strange chants were chanted; it was a weird music, like a litany of bumblebees. Dense clouds of incense issued from gilded recesses that were screened from view.

It was all very strange, very foreign, very unintelligible to us. It was also very monotonous; and when some of the unbelievers grew restless and stole quietly about on voyages of exploration and discovery, they were duly rewarded at the hands of the custodian of the chapel, who rather encouraged the seeming sacrilege. He left his prayers unsaid to pilot us from nook to nook; he exhibited the old paintings of Byzantine origin, and in broken English endeavored to interpret their meaning. He opened antique chests that we might examine their contents; and when a volume of prayers printed in rustic Russian type and bound with clumsy metal clasps, was bartered for, he seemed quite willing to dispose of it, though it was the only one of the kind visible on the premises. This excited our cupidity, and, with a purse in our hand, we groped into the sacristy seeking what we might secure.

A set of small chromos came to light: bright visions of the Madonna, done in three or four colors, on thin paper and fastened to blocks of wood. They were worth about two cents – perhaps three for five. We paid fifty cents apiece, and were glad to get them at that price – oh, the madness of the seeker after souvenirs! Then all unexpectedly we came upon a collection of half-obliterated panel paintings. They were thrown carelessly in a deep window-seat, and had been overlooked by many. They were Russian to the very grain of the wood; they were quaint to the verge of the ludicrous; they were positively black with age; thick layers of dust and dirt and smoke of incense coated them, so that the faint colors that were laid upon them were sunk almost out of sight. The very wood itself was weather-stained, and a chip out of it left no trace of life or freshness beneath. Centuries old they seemed, these small panels, sacred *Ikons*. In far-away Russia they may have been venerated before this continent had verified the dream of Columbus. As we were breaking nearly all the laws of propriety, I thought it safe to inquire the price of these. I did so. Would I had been the sole one within hearing that I might have glutted my gorge on the spot! They were fifteen cents apiece, and they were divided among us as ruthlessly as if they were the seamless shirt of blessed memory.

Meanwhile the ceremonies at the high altar had come to an end. The amiable assistant of Father Mitropolski was displaying the treasures of the sanctuary with pardonable pride, – jewelled crosiers, golden chalices, robes resplendent with rubies, amethysts and pearls, paintings upon ivory, and images clothed in silver and precious stones. The little chapel, cruciform, is decorated in white and gold; the altar screens are of bronze set with images of silver. Soft carpets of the Orient were spread upon the steps of the altar.

How pretty it all seemed as we turned to leave the place and saw everything dimly in the blue vapor that still sweetened and hallowed it! And when the six bells in the belfry all fell to ringing riotously, and the sun let slip a few stray beams that painted the spire a richer green, and the grassy street that stretches from the church porch to the shore was dotted with groups of strollers, St Michael's at Sitka, in spite of its dingy and unsymmetrical exterior, seemed to us one of the prettiest spots it had ever been our lot to see.

It is a grassy and a mossy town that gathers about the Russian chapel. All the old houses were built to last (as they are likely to do) for many generations to come. They are log-houses – the public buildings, the once fashionable officers' club, and many of the residences, – formed of solid square brown logs laid one upon another until you come to the roof. At times the logs are clapboarded without, and are all lathed and plastered within. The floors are solid and the stairs also. The wonder is how the town can ever go to ruin – save by fire; for wood doesn't rot in Alaska, but will lie in logs exposed to the changes of the season for an indefinite period.

I saw in a wood back of the town an immense log. It was in the primeval forest, and below it were layers of other logs lying crosswise and in confusion. I know not how far below me was the solid earth, for mats of thick moss and deep beds of dead leaves filled the hollows between the logs; but this log, nearly three feet in diameter, was above them all; and out of it – from a seed no doubt imbedded in the bark – had sprung a tree that is to-day as great in girth as the log that lies prostrate beneath its roots. These mighty roots have clasped that log in an everlasting embrace and struck down into the soil below. You can conjecture how long the log has been lying there in that tangle of mighty roots – yet the log is to-day as sound a bit of timber as one is likely to find anywhere.

Alaska is buried under forests like these – I mean that part of it which is not still cased in ice and snow. A late official gave me out of his cabinet a relic of the past. It is a stone pestle, rudely but symmetrically hewn, – evidently the work of the aborigines. This pestle, with several stone implements of domestic utility, was discovered by a party of prospectors who had dug under the roots of a giant tree. Eleven feet beneath the surface, directly under the tree and surrounded by gigantic roots, this pestle, and some others of a similar character, together with mortars and various utensils, were scattered through the soil. Most of the collection went to the Smithsonian Institute, and perhaps their origin and history may be some day conjectured. How many ages more, I wonder, will be required to develop the resources of this vast out-of-door country?

When the tardy darkness fell upon Sitka – toward midnight – the town was hardly more silent than it had been throughout the day. A few lights were twinkling in distant windows; a few Indians were prowling about; the water rippled along the winding shore; and from time to time as the fresh gusts blew in from the sea, some sleepless bird sailed over us on shadowy wings, and uttered a half-smothered cry that startled the listener. Then, indeed, old Sitka, which was once called New Archangel, seemed but a relic of the past, whose vague, romantic history will probably never be fully known.

# CHAPTER XIII

## Katalan's Rock

Katalan's Rock towers above the sea at the top corner of Sitka. Below it, on the one hand, the ancient colonial houses are scattered down the shore among green lawns like pasture lands, and beside grass-grown streets with a trail of dust in the middle of them. On the other hand, the Siwash Indian lodges are clustered all along the beach. This rancheria was originally separated from the town by a high stockade, and the huge gates were closed at night for the greater security of the inhabitants; but since the American occupation the gates have been destroyed, and only a portion of the stockade remains.

Katalan's Rock is steep enough to command the town, and ample enough to afford all the space necessary for fortifications and the accommodation of troops and stores. A natural Gibraltar, it was the site of the first settlement, and has ever remained the most conspicuous and distinguished quarter of the colony.

The first building erected on this rock was a block-house, which was afterward burned. A second building, reared on the ruins of the first, was destroyed by an earthquake; but a third, the colonial castle and residence of the governors, stands to this day. It crowns the summit of the rock, is one hundred and forty feet in length, seventy feet in depth, two stories with basement and attic, and has a lookout that commands one of the most romantic and picturesque combinations of land and sea imaginable.

It is not a handsome edifice, nor is it in the least like a castle, nor like what one supposes a castle should be. Were it anywhere else, it might pass for the country residence of a gentleman of the old school, or for an unfashionable suburban hotel, or for a provincial seminary. It is built of solid cedar logs that seem destined to weather the storms of ages. These logs are secured by innumerable copper bolts; and the whole structure is riveted to the rocks, so that neither wind nor wave nor earthquake shock is likely to prevail against it.

Handsomely finished within, it was in the colonial days richly furnished; and as Sitka was at that time a large settlement composed of wealthy and highbred Russians, governed by a prince or a baron whose petty court was made up of the representatives of the rank and fashion of St. Petersburg and Moscow, the colonial castle was most of the time the scene of social splendor.

The fame of the brilliant and beautiful Baroness Wrangell, first chatelaine of the castle, lives after her. She was succeeded by the wife of Governor Kupreanoff, a brave lady, who in 1835 crossed Siberia on horseback to Behring Sea on her way to Sitka. Later the Princess Maksontoff became the social queen, and reigned in the little castle on Katalan's Rock as never queen reigned before. A flagship was anchored under the windows, and the proud Admiral spent much of his time on shore. The officers' clubhouse, yonder down the grassy street, was the favorite lounging place of the navy. The tea-gardens have run to seed, and the race-course is obliterated, where, doubtless, fair ladies and brave men disported themselves in the interminable twilights of the Alaskan summer. In the reign of the Princess Maksontoff the ladies were first shown to the sideboard. When they had regaled themselves with potent punch and caviare, the gentlemen followed suit. But the big brazen samovar was forever steaming in the grand salon, and delicious draughts of caravan tea were in order at all hours.

What days they were, when the castle was thronged with guests, and those of all ages and descriptions and from every rank in and out of society! The presidential levee is not more democratic than were the *fétes* of the Princess Maksontoff. To the music of the Admiral's band combined with the castle orchestra, it was "all hands round." The Prince danced with each and every lady in turn. The Princess was no less gracious, for all danced with her who chose, from the Lord High Admiral to midshipmite and the crew of the captain's gig.

You will read of these things in the pages of Lutka, Sir George Simpson, Sir Edward Belcher, and other early voyagers. They vouch for the unique charm of the colonial life at that day. Washington Irving, in his "Astoria," has something to say of New Archangel (Michael), or "Sheetka," as he spells it; but it is of the time when the ships of John Jacob Astor were touching in that vicinity, and the reports are not so pleasing.

While social life in the little colony was still more enjoyable, a change came that in a single hour reversed the order of affairs. For years Russia had been willing, if not eager, to dispose of the great lands that lay along the northwestern coast of America. She seemed never to have cared much for them, nor to have believed much in their present value or possible future development. No enterprise was evinced among the people: they were comparative exiles, who sought to relieve the monotony of their existence by one constant round of gaity. *Soirées* at the castle, tea-garden parties, picnics upon the thousand lovely isles that beautify the Sitkan Sea; strolls among the sylvan retreats in which the primeval forest, at the very edge of the town, abounds; fishing and hunting expeditions, music, dancing, lively conversation, strong punch, caviare and the steaming samovar, – those were the chief diversions with which noble and serf alike sought to lighten the burden of the day.

While Russia was willing to part with the lone land on the Pacific, she was determined that it should not pass into the hands of certain of the powers for whom she had little or no love. Hence there was time for the United States to consider the question of a purchase and to haggle a little over the price. For years the bargain hung in the balance. When it was finally settled, it was settled so suddenly that the witnesses had to be wakened and called out of their beds. They assembled secretly, in the middle of the night, as if they were conspirators; and before sunrise the whole matter was fixed forever.

On the 18th of October, 1867, three United States ships of war anchored off Katalan's Rock. These were the Ossipee, the Jamestown and the Resaca. In the afternoon, at half-past three o'clock, the terrace before the castle was surrounded by United States troops, Russian soldiers, officials, citizens and Indians. The town was alive with Russian bunting, and the ships aflutter with Stars and Stripes and streamers. There was something ominous in the air and in the sunshine. Bang! went the guns from the Ossipee, and the Russian flag slowly descended from the lofty staff on the castle; but the wind caught it and twisted it round and round the staff, and it was long before a boatswain's chair could be rigged to the halyards, and some one hauled up to disentangle the rebellious banner.

Meanwhile the rain began to fall, and the Princess Maksontoff was in tears. It was a dismal hour for the proud court of the doughty governor. The Russian water battery was firing a salute from the dock as the Stars and Stripes were climbing to the skies – the great continent of icy peaks and pine was passing from the hands of one nation to the other. In the silence that ensued, Captain Pestehouroff stepped forward and said: "By authority of his Majesty the Emperor of Russia, I transfer to the

United States the Territory of Alaska." The prince governor then surrendered his insignia of office, and the thing was done. In a few months' time fifty ships and four hundred people had deserted Sitka; and to-day but three families of pure Russian blood remain. Perhaps the fault-finding which followed this remarkable acquisition of territory on the part of the United States government – both the acquisition and the fault-finding were on the part of our government – had best be left unmentioned. Now that the glorious waters of that magnificent archipelago have become the resort of summer tourists, every man, woman and child can see for his, her and its self; and this is the only way in which to convince an American of anything.

Thirty years ago Sitka was what I have attempted to describe above. To-day how different! Passing its barracks at the foot of Katalan's Rock, one sees a handful of marines looking decidedly bored if off duty. The steps that lead up to the steep incline of the rock to the castle terrace are fast falling to decay. Weeds and rank grass trail over them and cover the whole top of the rock. The castle has been dismantled. The walls will stand until they are blown up or torn down, but all traces of the original ornamentation of the interior have disappeared. The carved balustrades, the curious locks, knobs, hinges, chandeliers, and fragments of the wainscoting, have been borne away by enterprising curio hunters. There was positively nothing left for me to take.

One may still see the chamber occupied by Secretary Seward, who closed the bargain with the Russian Government at $7,200,000, cash down. Lady Franklin occupied that chamber when she was scouring these waters in the fearless and indefatigable, but fruitless, search for the relics of the lost Sir John. One handsome apartment has been partially restored and suitably furnished for the use of the United States District Attorney. Two rooms on the groundfloor are occupied by the signal officers; but the rest of the building is in a shameful condition, and only its traditions remain to make it an object of interest to every stranger guest.

It is said that twice in the year, at the dead hour of the night, the ghost of a bride wanders sorrowfully from room to room. She was the daughter of one of the old governors – a stern parent, who forced her into a marriage without love. On the bridal eve, while all the guests were assembled, and the bride, in wedding garments, was the centre of attraction, she suddenly disappeared. After a long search her body was found in one of the apartments of the castle, but life was extinct. At Eastertide the shade of this sad body makes the round of the deserted halls, and in passing leaves after it a faint odor of wild roses.

The basement is half filled with old rubbish. I found rooms where an amateur minstrel entertainment had been given. Rude lettering upon the walls recorded the fact in lampblack, and a monster hand pointed with index finger to its temporary bar. Burnt-cork *débris* was scattered about, and there were "old soldiers" enough on the premises to have quite staggered a moralist. The Muscovite reign is over. The Princess is in her grave on the hill yonder, – a grave that was forgotten for a time and lost in the jungle that has overgrown the old Russian cemetery. The Indians mutilated that tomb; but Lieutenant Gilman, in charge of the marines attached to the Adams, restored it; and he, with his men, did much toward preserving Sitka from going to the dogs.

Gone are the good old days, but the Americanized Sitka does not propose to be behind the times. I discovered a theatre. It was in one of the original Russian houses, doomed to last forever – a long, narrow hall, with a stage at the upper end of it. A few scenes, evidently painted on the spot and in dire distress; a drop-curtain depicting an utterly impracticable roseate ice-gorge in the ideal Alaska, and four footlights, constituted the sum total of the properties. The stage was six feet deep, about ten feet broad, and the "flies" hung like "bangs" above the foreheads of the players. In the next room, convenient in case of a panic, was the Sitka fire department, consisting of a machine of one-man-power, which a small boy might work without endangering anybody or anything.

Suburban Sitka is sweet and sad. One passes on the way to the wildwood, where everybody goes as often as may be, – a so-called "blarney stone." Many a fellow has chipped away at that stone while he chatted with his girl – I suppose that is where the blarney comes in, – and left his name or initials for a sacred memory. There are dull old Russian hieroglyphs there likewise. Love is alike in all languages, you know. The truth about the stone is merely this: it is a big soft stone by the sea, and of just the right height to rest a weary pilgrim. There old Baranoff, the first governor, used to sit of a summer afternoon and sip his Russian brandy until he was as senseless as the stone beneath him; and then he was carried in state up to the colonial castle and suffered to sober off.

Beyond the stone, and the curving beach with the grass-grown highway skirting it, is the forest; and through this forest is the lovers' lane, made long ago by the early colonists and kept in perfect trim by the latest, – a lane that is green-arched overhead and fern-walled on either side, and soft with the dust of dead pine boughs underfoot. There also are streams and waterfalls and rustic bridges such as one might look for in some stately park in England, but hardly in Alaska. Surely there is no bit of wilderness finer than this. All is sweet and grave and silent, save for the ripple of waters and the sighing of winds.

As for the Siwash village on the other side of Sitka, it is a Siwash village over again. How soon one wearies of them! But one ought never to weary of the glorious sea isles and the overshadowing mountains that lie on every side of the quaint, half-barbarous capital. Though it is dead to the core and beginning to show the signs of death, it is one of the dreamiest spots on earth, and just the one for long summer solitude, – at least so we all thought, for on the morrow we were homeward bound.

# CHAPTER XIV

# From the Far North

Sitka is the turning-point in the Alaskan summer cruise. It is the beginning of the end; and I am more than half inclined to think that in most cases – charming as the voyage is and unique in its way beyond any other voyage within reach of the summer tourist – the voyager is glad of it. One never gets over the longing for some intelligence from the outer world; never quite becomes accustomed to the lonely, far-away feeling that at times is a little painful and often is a bore.

During the last hours at Sitka, Mount Edgecombe loomed up gloriously, and reminded one of Fugjyamma. It is a very handsome and a highly ornamental mountain. So are the islands that lie between it and the Sitkan shore handsome and ornamental, but there are far too many of them. The picture is overcrowded, and in this respect is as unlike the Bay of Naples as possible; though some writers have compared them, and of course, as is usual in cases of comparison, to the disadvantage of the latter.

Leaving Sitka, we ran out to sea. It was much easier to do this than go a long way round among the islands; and, as the weather was fair, the short cut was delightful. We rocked like a cradle – the *Ancon* rocks like a cradle on the slightest provocation. The sea sparkled, the wavelets leaped and clapped their hands. Once in awhile a plume of spray was blown over the bow, and the delicate stomach recoiled upon itself suggestively; but the deliciousness of the air in the open sea and the brevity of the cruise – we were but five or six hours outside – kept us in a state of intense delight. Presently we ran back into the maze of fiords and land-locked lakes, and resumed the same old round of daily and nightly experiences.

Juneau, Douglas Island, Fort Wrangell, and several fishing stations were revisited. They seemed a little stale to us, and we were inclined to snub them slightly. Of course we thought we knew it all – most of us knew as much as we cared to know; and so we strolled leisurely about the solemn little settlements, and, no doubt, but poorly succeeded in disguising the superior air which distinguishes the new arrival in a strange land. It is but a step from a state of absolute greenness on one's arrival at a new port to a *blasé* languor, wherein nothing can touch one further; and the step is easily and usually taken inside of a week. May the old settlers forgive us our idiocy!

There was a rainy afternoon at Fort Wrangell, – a very proper background, for the place is dismal to a degree. An old stern-wheel steamboat, beached in the edge of the village, was used as a hotel during the decline of the gold fever; but while the fever was at its height the boat is said to have cleared $135,000 per season. The coolie has bored into its hollow shell and washes there, clad in a semi-Boyton suit of waterproof.

I made my way through the dense drizzle to the Indian village at the far end of the town. The untrodden streets are grass-grown; and a number of the little houses, gray with weather stains, are deserted and falling to decay. Reaching a point of land that ran out and lost itself in mist, I found a few Indians smoking and steaming, as they sat in the damp sand by their canoes.

A long footbridge spans a strip of tide land. I ventured to cross it, though it looked as if it would blow away in the first gust of wind. It was a long, long bridge, about broad enough for a single passenger; yet I was met in the middle of it by a well-blanketed squaw, bound inland. It was a question in my mind whether it were better to run and leap lightly over her, since we must pass on a single rail, or to lie down and allow her to climb over me. O happy inspiration! In the mist and the rain, in the midst of that airy path, high above the mud flats, and with the sullen tide slowly sweeping in from the gray wastes beyond the capes, I seized my partner convulsively, and with our toes together we swung as on a pivot and went our ways rejoicing.

The bridge led to the door of a chief's house, and the door stood open. It was a large, square house, of one room only, and with the floor sunk to the depth of three feet in the centre. It was like looking into a dry swimming bath. A step, or terrace, on the four sides of the room made the descent easy, and I descended. The chief, in a cast-off military jacket, gave me welcome with a mouthful of low gutterals. I found a good stove in the lodge and several comfortable-looking beds, with chintz curtains and an Oriental superabundance of pillows. A few photographs in cheap frames adorned the walls; a few flaming chromos – Crucifixions and the like – hung there, along with fathoms of fishnet, clusters of fish-hooks, paddles, kitchen furniture, wearing apparel, and a blunderbuss or two. Four huge totem poles, or ponderous carvings, supported the heavy beams of the roof in the manner of caryatides. These figures, half veiled in shadow, were most impressive, and gave a kind of Egyptian solemnity to the dimly lighted apartment.

The chief was not alone. His man Friday was with him, and together we sat and smoked in a silence that was almost suffocating. It fairly snapped once or twice, it was so dense; and then we three exchanged grave smiles and puffed away in great contentment. The interview was brought to a sudden close by the chief's making me a very earnest offer of $6 for my much-admired gum ulster, and I refusing it with scorn – for it was still raining. So we parted coldly, and I once more walked the giddy bridge with fear and trembling; for I am not a somnambulist, who alone might perform there with impunity.

It was a bad day for curios. The town had been sacked on the voyage up; yet I prowled in these quarters, where one would least expect to find treasure, inasmuch as it is mostly found just there. Presently the most hideous of faces was turned up at me from the threshold of a humble lodge. It was of a dead green color, with blood trimmings; the nose beaked like a parrot's, the mouth a gaping crescent; the eyeless sockets seemed to sparkle and blink with inner eyes set in the back of the skull; murderous scalp locks streamed over the ill-shapen brow; and from the depths of this monstrosity some one, or something, said, "Boo!" I sprang backward, only to hear the gurgle of baby laughter, and see the wee face of a half-Indian cherub peering from behind the mask. Well, that mask is mine now; and whenever I look at it I think of the falling dusk in Fort Wrangell, and of the child on all-fours who startled me on my return from the chief's house beyond the bridge, and who cried as if her little heart would break when I paid for her plaything and cruelly bore it away.

Some of the happiest hours of the voyage were the "wee sma'" ones, when I lounged about the deserted deck with Captain George, the pilot. A gentleman of vast experience and great reserve, for years he has haunted that archipelago; he knows it in the dark, and it was his nightly duty to pace the deck while the ship was almost as still as death. He has heard the great singers of the past, the queens of song whose voices were long since hushed. We talked of these in the vast silence of the Alaskan night, and of the literature of the sea, and especially of that solitary northwestern sea, while we picked our way among the unpeopled islands that crowded all about us.

On such a night, while we were chatting

in low voices as we leaned over the quarter-rail, and the few figures that still haunted the deck were like veritable ghosts, Captain George seized me by the arm and exclaimed: "Look there!" I looked up into the northern sky. There was not a cloud visible in all that wide expanse, but something more filmy than a cloud floated like a banner among the stars. It might almost have been a cobweb stretched from star to star – each strand woven from a star beam, – but it was ever changing in form and color. Now it was scarf-like, fluttering and waving in a gentle breeze; and now it hung motionless – a deep fringe of lace gathered in ample folds. Anon it opened suddenly from the horizon, and spread in panels like a fan that filled the heavens. As it opened and shut and swayed to and fro as if it were a fan in motion, it assumed in turn all the colors of the rainbow, but with a delicacy of tint and texture even beyond that of the rainbow. Sometimes it was like a series of transparencies – shadow pictures thrown upon the screen of heaven, lit by a light beyond it – the mysterious light we know not of. That is what the pilot and I saw while most of the passengers were sleeping. It was the veritable *aurora borealis*, and that alone were worth the trip to Alaska.

One day we came to Fort Tongass – a port of entry, and our last port in the great, lone land – for all the way down through the British possessions we touch no land until we reach Victoria or Nanaimo. Tongass was once a military post, and now has the unmistakable air of a desert island. Some of us were not at all eager to go on shore. You see, we were beginning to get our fill of this monotonous out-of-the-world and out-of-the-way life. Yet Tongass is unique, and certainly has the most interesting collection of totem poles that one is likely to see on the voyage. At Tongass there is a little curving beach, where the ripples sparkle among the pebbles. Beyond the beach is a strip of green lawn, and at the top of the lawn the old officers' quarters, now falling to decay. For background there are rocks and trees and the sea. The sea is everywhere about Tongass, and the sea-breezes blow briskly, and the sea-gulls waddle about the lawn and sit in rows upon the sagging roofs as if they were thoroughly domesticated. Oh, what a droll place it is!

After a little deliberation we all went ashore in several huge boat-loads; and, to our surprise, were welcomed by a charming young bride in white muslin and ribbons of baby-blue. Somehow she had found her way to the desert island – or did she spring up there like a wild flower? And the grace with which she did the honors was the subject of unbounded praise during the remainder of the voyage.

This pretty Bret Harte heroine, with all of the charms and virtues and none of the vices of his camp-followers, led us through the jagged rocks of the dilapidated quarters, down among the spray-wet rocks on the other side of the island, and all along the dreary waste that fronts the Indian village. Oh, how dreary that waste is! – the rocks, black and barren, and scattered far into the frothing sea; the sandy path along the front of the Indian lodges, with rank grass shaking and shivering in the wind; the solemn and grim array of totem poles standing in front or at the sides of the weather-stained lodges – and the whole place deserted. I know not where the Indians had gone, but they were not there – save a sick squaw or two. Probably, being fishermen, the tribe had gone out with their canoes, and were now busy with the spoils somewhere among the thousand passages of the archipelago.

The totem poles at Tongass are richly carved, brilliantly colored, and grotesque in the extreme. Some of the lodges were roomy but sad-looking, and with a perpetual shade hovering through them. We found inscriptions in English – very rudely lettered – on many of the lodges and totem poles: "In memory of" some one or another chief or notable red-man. Over one door was this inscription: "In memory of ----, who died by his own hand." The lodge door was fastened with a rusty padlock, and the place looked ghoulish.

I think we were all glad to get out of Tongass, though we received our best welcome there. At any rate, we sat on the beach and got our feet wet and our pockets full of sand waiting for the deliberate but dead-sure boatmen to row us to the ship. When we steamed away we left the little bride in her desert island to the serene and sacred joy of her honeymoon, hoping that long before it had begun to wane she might return to the world; for in three brief weeks we were beginning to lust after it. That evening we anchored in a well-wooded cove and took on several lighter-loads of salmon casks. Captain Carroll and the best shots in the ship passed the time in shooting at a barrel floating three hundred yards distant. So ran our little world away, as we were homeward bound and rapidly nearing the end of the voyage.

# CHAPTER XV

## Out of the Arctic

When Captain Cook – who, with Captain Kidd, nearly monopolizes the young ladies' ideal romance of the seas – was in these waters, he asked the natives what land it was that lay about them, and they replied: "Alaska" – great land. It *is* a great land, lying loosely along the northwest coast, – great in area, great in the magnitude and beauty of its forests and in the fruitfulness of its many waters; great in the splendor of its ice fields; the majesty of its rivers, the magnificence of its snow-clad peaks; great also in its possibilities, and greatest of all in its measureless wealth of gold.

In the good old days of the Muscovite reign – 1811, – Governor Baranoff sent Alexander Kuskoff to establish a settlement in California where grain and vegetables might be raised for the Sitka market. The ruins of Fort Ross are all that remain to tell the tale of that enterprise. The Sitkan of to-day manages to till a kitchen-garden that suffices; but his wants are few, and then he can always fall back on canned provision if his fresh food fails.

The stagnation of life in Alaska is all but inconceivable. The summer tourist can hardly realize it, because he brings to the settlement the only variety it knows; and this comes so seldom – once or twice a month – that the population arises as a man and rejoices so long as the steamer is in port. Please to picture this people after the excitement is over, quietly subsiding into a comatose state, and remaining in it until the next boat heaves in sight. One feeds one's self mechanically; takes one's constitutional along the shore or over one of the goat-paths that strike inland; nodding now and again to the familiar faces that seem never to change in expression except during tourist's hours; and then repairs to that bed which is the salvation of the solitary, for sleep and oblivion are the good angels that brood over it. In summer the brief night – barely forty winks in length – is so silvery and so soft that it is a delight to sit up in it even if one is alone. Lights and shadows play with one another, and are reflected in sea and sky until the eye is almost dazzled with the loveliness of the scene. I believe if I were banished to Alaska I would sleep in the daytime – say from 8 a. m. to 5 p. m., – and revel in the wakeful beauty of the other hours.

But the winter, and the endless night of winter! – when the sun sinks to rest in discouragement at three or four o'clock in the afternoon, and rises with a faint heart and a pale face at ten or eleven in the forenoon; when even high noon is unworthy of the name – for the dull luminary, having barely got above the fence at twelve o'clock, backs out of it and sinks again into the blackness of darkness one is destined to endure for at least two thirds of the four and twenty! Since the moon is no more obliging to the Alaskans than the sun is, what is a poor fellow to do? He can watch the aurora until his eyes ache; he can sit over a game of cards and a glass of toddy – he can always get the latter up there; he can trim his lamp and chat with his chums and fill his pipe over and over again. But the night thickens and the time begins to lag; he looks at his watch, to find it is only 9 p. m., and there are twelve hours between him and daylight. It is a great land in which to store one's mind with knowledge, provided one has the books at hand and good eyes and a lamp that won't flicker or smoke. Yet why should I worry about this when there are people who live through it and like it? – or at least they say they do.

In my mind's eye I see the Alaska of the future – and the not far-distant future. Among the most beautiful of the islands there will be fine openings; lawns and flowers will carpet the slopes from the dark walls of the forest to the water's edge. In the midst of these favored spots summer hotels will throw wide their glorious windows upon vistas that are like glimpses of fairy land. Along the beach numerous skiffs await those who are weary of towns; steam launches are there, and small barges for the transportation of picnic parties to undiscovered islands in the dim distance. Sloop yachts with the more adventurous will go forth on voyages of exploration and discovery, two or three days in length, under the guidance of stolid, thoroughbred Indian pilots. There may be an occasional wreck, with narrow escapes from the watery grave – let us hope so, for the sake of variety. There will be fishing parties galore, and camping on foreign shores, and eagle hunts, and the delights of the chase; with Indian retinues and Chinese cooks, and the "swell toggery" that is the chief, if not the only, charm of that sort of thing. There will be circulating libraries in each hotel, and grand pianos, and private theatricals, and nightly hops that may last indefinitely, or at least until sunrise, without shocking the most prudent; for day breaks at 2 a. m.

There will be visits from one hotel to the other, and sea-voyages to dear old Sitka, where the Grand Hotel will be located; and there will be the regular weekly or semi-weekly boat to the Muir glacier, with professional guides to the top of it, and all the necessary traps furnished on board if desired. And this wild life can begin as early as April and go on until the end of September without serious injury. There will be no hay fever or prickly-heat; neither will there be sunstrokes nor any of the horrors of the

Eastern and Southern summer. It will remain true to its promise of sweet, warm days, and deliciously cool evenings, in which the young lover may woo his fair to the greatest advantage; for there is no night there. Then everyone will come home with a new experience, which is the best thing one can come home with, and the rarest nowadays; and with a pocketful of Alaskan garnets, which are about the worst he can come home with, being as they are utterly valueless, and unhandsome even when they are beautifully symmetrical.

Oh, the memory of the voyage, which is perhaps the most precious of all! – this we bring home with us forever. The memory of all that is half civilized and wholly unique and uncommon: of sleepy and smoky wigwams, where the ten tribes hold powwow in a confusion of gutturals, with a plentiful mixture of saliva; for it is a moist language, a gurgle that approaches a gargle, and in three weeks the unaccustomed ear scarcely recovers from the first shock of it; a memory of totem poles in stark array, and of the high feast in the Indian villages, where the beauty and chivalry of the forest gathered and squatted in wide circles listening to some old-man-eloquent in the very ecstasy of expectoration; the memory of a non-committing, uncommunicative race, whose religion is a feeble polytheism – a kind of demonolatry; for, as good spirits do not injure one, one's whole time is given to the propitiation of the evil. This is called Shamanism, and is said to have been the religion of the Tartar race before the introduction of Buddhism, and is still the creed of the Siberians; a memory of solitary canoes on moonlit seas and of spicy pine odors mingled with the tonic of moist kelp and salt-sea air.

A memory of friends who were altogether charming, of a festival without a flaw. O my kind readers! when the Alaska Summer Hotel Company has stocked the nooks and corners of the archipelago with caravansaries, and good boats are filling them with guests who go to spend the season in the far Northwest, fail not to see that you are numbered among the elect; for Alaska outrivers all rivers and out-lakes all lakes – being itself a lake of ten thousand islands; it out-mountains the Alps of America, and certainly outdoes everything else everywhere else, in the shape of a watering place. And when you have returned from there, after two or three months' absence from the world and its weariness, you will begin to find that your "tum-tum is white" for the first time since your baptismal day, and that you have gained enough in strength and energy to topple the totem pole of your enemy without shedding a feather. There is hope for Alaska in the line of a summer resort.

As ghosts scent the morning air and are dispersed, so we scented the air, which actually seemed more familiar as we approached Washington in the great Northwest; and the spirit of peace, of ease and of lazy contentment that had possessed our souls for three weeks took flight. It was now but a day's sail to Victoria, and yet we began to think we would never get there.

We were hungry for news of the world which we had well-nigh forgotten. Three weeks! It seemed to us that in this little while cities might have been destroyed, governments overthrown, new islands upheaved and old ones swallowed out of sight. Then we were all expecting to find heaps of letters from everybody awaiting us at Victoria or Port Townsend, and our mouths fairly watered for news.

We took a little run into the sea and got lost in a fog; but the pilot whistled for the landmarks, and Echo answered; so that by the time the fog was ready to roll away, like a snowy drop-curtain, we knew just where we were, and ran quietly into a nook that looked as if it would fit us like a bootjack. The atmosphere grew smoky; forest fires painted the sky with burnt umber, and through this veil the sun shone like a copper shield. Then a gorgeous moonlight followed. There was blood upon that moon, and all the shores were like veins in moss-agate and the sea like oil. We wound in and out, in and out, among dreamy islands; touched for a little while at Nanaimo, where we should have taken in a cargo of coal for Portland, whither the *Ancon* was bound; but Captain Carroll kindly put us all

173

ashore first and then returned for his freight.

We hated to sleep that night, and did not sleep very much. But when we awakened it was uncommonly quiet; and upon going on deck – lo! we were at Victoria. What a quiet, pretty spot! What a restful and temperate climate! What jutting shores, soft hills, fine drives, old-countrified houses and porters' lodges and cottages, with homely flowers in the door-yards and homely people in the doors! – homely I mean in the handsomest sense, for I can not imagine the artificial long survives in that community.

How dear to us seemed civilization after our wanderings in the wilderness! We bought newspapers and devoured them; ran in and out of shops just for the fun of it and because our liberty was so dear to us then. News? We were fairly staggered with the abundance of it, and exchanged it with one another in the most fraternal fashion, sharing our joys and sorrows with the whole ship's company. And deaths? What a lot of these, and how startling when they come so unexpectedly and in such numbers! Why is it, I wonder, that so many people die when we are away somewhere beyond reach of communication?

But enough of this. A few jolly hours on shore, a few drives in the suburbs and strolls in the town, and we headed for Port Townsend and the United States, where we parted company with the good old ship that carried us safely to and fro. And there we ended the Alaskan voyage gladly enough, but not without regret; for, though uneventful, I can truly say it was one of the pleasantest voyages of my life; and one that – thanks to every one who shared it with me – I shall ever remember with unalloyed delight.

THE END.

Lightning Source UK Ltd.
Milton Keynes UK
175766UK00001B/57/P